Life is fu...

Stepping ou... a vase containing three fresh flowers on her desk. This time the arrangement consisted of a red fascia, a yellow daisy mum, and a white carnation. Only two words appeared on the card. "Guess who?" The answer didn't take much guesswork.

She set the flowers aside and immediately started working. Before long, Robert appeared beside her with more work.

"More flowers?"

Cindy mumbled her affirmation as she took the file from his hand and immediately started typing.

Robert stayed beside her. "He told me he wants to take you out to say thank you."

She made a typo and backspaced over it. "I know," she mumbled, trying to concentrate on the client's contract. "But, I told him just to send me a few flowers, so he did. I'm sure he'll soon forget about me."

"Maybe," Robert mumbled, studying the flowers. "Maybe not."

GAIL SATTLER lives in Vancouver, BC (where you don't have to shovel rain) with her husband, three sons, dog, and countless fish, many of which have names. She writes inspirational romance because she loves happily-ever-afters and believes God has a place in that happy ending. Visit Gail's website at http://www.gailsattler.com.

Books by Gail Sattler

HEARTSONG PRESENTS
HP269—Walking the Dog
HP306—Piano Lessons
HP325—Gone Camping
HP358—At Arm's Length
HP385—On the Road Again
HP397—My Name Is Mike
HP406—Almost Twins

A Few
Flowers

Gail Sattler

Heartsong Presents

Dedicated to my husband, Tim, who in some way is part of the hero in all my books. I love you, Sweetie!

A note from the author:
I love to hear from my readers! You may correspond with me by writing:
Gail Sattler
Author Relations
PO Box 719
Uhrichsville, OH 44683

ISBN 1-58660-259-4

A FEW FLOWERS

All Scripture quotations, unless otherwise indicated, are taken from the HOLY BIBLE, NEW INTERNATIONAL VERSION®. NIV®. Copyright © 1973, 1978, 1984 by International Bible Society. Used by permission of Zondervan Publishing House. All rights reserved.

All of the characters and events in this book are fictitious. Any resemblance to actual persons, living or dead, or to actual events is purely coincidental.

Cover illustration by Kay Salem.

PRINTED IN THE U.S.A.

prologue

Cindy wiped her damp brow and reached for her set of precision screwdrivers. The hot and humid warehouse did nothing but aggravate the tense atmosphere, and the noise grated constantly on her nerves. Still, she couldn't survive without the income, so she would suffer through until she could find employment elsewhere. This stint on the assembly line had to rank as the worst job she'd ever held.

A booming male voice interrupted her thoughts. "Cindy, can I see you, please?"

She followed Troy to his office, where he motioned her to sit in the chair across from him as he took his seat behind his large desk. "You don't like it here, do you?"

Cindy sucked in a deep breath and her heart thudded in her chest. Not yet over her probation, if management decided to terminate her, she would be without recourse. After being unemployed for too long, her savings had almost run out and she'd had to take in a roommate. She couldn't afford to lose this job.

Cindy gulped and gripped the arms of the chair. "I suppose the job isn't the most fulfilling one I've ever had, but I do my best," she said more calmly than she thought her shaking insides would allow.

"I see." He folded his hands on the desk in front of him.

She was sunk. She felt sure he was going to fire her. And she didn't even know why.

"Can you type?"

"Well, a little. Yes. . ."

"Have you ever worked in an office?"

"Uh, no. . ." Cindy's stomach churned. Her boss was suggesting something he thought she might be better suited for before he let the ax fall.

"I've been watching you, and while you're doing a fine job, I know you're not happy here. The senior vice president's secretary called in sick four days in a row, and today she just quit. The desk is in a state of anarchy and Robert Blackmore needs someone immediately. No one else from the secretarial pool. . ." The corners of his mouth tilted upward, and he cleared his throat. ". . .can be spared. All you have to do is answer the phone and do some typing until they find someone to take the job on a permanent basis."

Cindy struggled to keep her mouth from hanging open. Troy wasn't talking about just any secretarial position. He was talking about a job that required more experience than she had, by far.

She glanced down at her clothes, including her favorite beat-up, old sneakers. Her grease-streaked jeans had a hole in the knee, and her hair was caked with dirt after a trip to the bowels of the parts warehouse.

"Well?"

She met his stony stare. She'd already decided to look for another job anyway, and answering the phone wasn't beyond her capabilities.

Mustering up all her courage, she wiped her sweaty palms on her jeans. "Okay, I'll do it."

Troy stood. "Sit on a towel to keep their precious chair clean if you need to. Robert Blackmore said he's desperate, so I told him I would pull someone from the assembly line. Report upstairs in half an hour."

Troy opened the door and waited for her to leave. As Cindy approached, he extended his hand. "I hope this works out for you."

Her head reeled at what sounded like a permanent good-bye. She merely nodded and weakly returned his handshake. To her surprise, he held on when she tried to pull away. "I'm warning you right now. Don't ever let Blackmore know what you did before you started working here."

At his words, Troy smiled and winked. Cindy nearly fainted. Before she said something really stupid, she hustled to the lunchroom, where she barely managed to choke down half a sandwich. She then hurried to the washroom and attempted to wipe off some of the morning's grime from her clothes.

At one o'clock, Cindy headed for the elevator.

On the seventh floor, the elevator door opened to a large, silent, thickly carpeted expanse. The heady aroma of fresh coffee wafted into the open compartment.

Cindy stood alone in the stopped elevator. Shiny brass lettering on the solid wooden doors of the company's top executives glittered in the bright fluorescent light. Four desks, aligned in a neat, professional row, sat beside the large window. One very untidy desk sat alone in front of the largest office on the floor.

She stepped out of the elevator, and the doors immediately swooshed closed behind her. Four well-dressed ladies with coffee cups in their hands approached. At the sight of her, they all stopped dead in their tracks.

"Hi," she mumbled, trying to show a confidence she did not feel. "I'm Cindy Martins. I'm here to temporarily fill the vacant desk."

The oldest lady of the group stepped forward. "My name is Ann, and this is Susan, Brenda, and Melinda." They all nodded at the mention of their names. "We're glad you volunteered, because, to tell the truth, we all refused to do it." She paused and turned to the messy desk while speaking to Cindy. "What did they tell you about the job?"

Cindy hesitated. "Troy said I only have to answer the phone and maybe do a little typing." Her smile faded as the three other ladies burst out laughing.

Before she had a chance to ask what was so funny, a heavyset, balding man in a navy suit opened the door of the large office next to the messy desk. He scowled at the desk, then at her. "You must be Cindy Martins. I've been expecting you," he said gruffly.

She approached him with as much grace as she could

muster. "And you must be Robert Blackmore. I'm pleased to meet you." She held out her hand, but instead of a handshake, he stared at the hole in her jeans. He thrust a file folder with papers sticking out at odd angles into Cindy's outstretched hand. "This is what I need first. I'm not taking calls until three o'clock unless it's my wife. I take my coffee black with one sugar." At that declaration, he turned back into his office and closed the door in her face.

Cindy couldn't believe his audacity. She at least expected a thank-you for agreeing to help.

Soft female giggling from the row of desks by the window interrupted her thoughts. "Do you see why none of us would do that job?" asked Susan. "You couldn't pay me enough to put up with him. That's why Elsie quit."

She looked at the bulging folder in her hand, then at the disorderly mountain of papers on the desk. It was this or the assembly line.

"Lots of luck, Cindy," Susan said. "You'll need all you can get."

She heard a string of nasty words, crystal clear even through Robert Blackmore's thick wooden door, then stared blankly at the desk that was to be hers for the rest of the week.

She had wanted another job. In the future she would be more careful about what she prayed for.

one

"Thanks for doing this for me on short notice, Troy."

"No problem. I might have fun being the victim of a beautiful woman."

Cindy shot him her best dirty look, but he only laughed. She'd almost forgotten that it was her turn to provide a volunteer for their monthly practice for the first aid competition. Maybe this year, they would beat City Tractor's team and claim the trophy.

"So, will this hurt?"

Cindy gulped down the last of her dinner. "Only your pride. You'll get some fake blood painted on you or, perhaps, some rearranged fake body parts. Maybe both."

Troy made a face and pushed his plate away. "Let me get this straight. You paint me and stick horror movie props on me, then poke and prod me while I'm lying on the ground pretending to be mortally wounded."

"Something like that."

"Brother. The things one does for a friend."

Cindy didn't comment. A short month ago, she could never have foreseen what had taken place. On top of the shock of actually getting the job on a permanent basis, she was even more shocked when she and Troy became such good friends so quickly. Now and then, he still tried to make more of their relationship, but she'd told him, in no uncertain terms, how she felt about him. In a way, even though she hated to admit it, she enjoyed his teasing and playful flirting. One day, when he met his "Miss Right," Cindy knew she would be sitting in the first row at his wedding crying her eyes out.

Troy checked his watch. "So tell me again. What am I supposed to do?"

"Jacques has everything set up in advance. He'll tell you, as the victim, what your injuries are. Go with it and use your imagination. In real life, every accident situation is unique and unpredictable. This is no different." She winked, but instead of taking the gesture the way she intended, Troy made a playful, low growl and reached for her hand. She slapped his fingers away. He pretended to pout.

"So I can do what I want?"

"Within reason. We try to determine your injuries and get you ready for transport."

He grasped himself around the throat and crossed his eyes. "Transport? Not to the morgue, I hope."

"No!" she laughed, then quieted when people from nearby tables turned to stare. "To the hospital. This is first aid. We just package you for the ambulance and the medical profession does the rest. After the meeting, we discuss our performance as a group, clean up, and go home."

"What a great evening out. Wish I'd thought of it. Why are you doing this?"

Cindy sighed. "There's no better way to practice industrial first aid. It's a good way to help with the refresher courses I need to maintain my certificate."

"But you don't need industrial first aid to be an executive secretary. That is, unless Blackmore falls off his fat—"

"Troy!! You know how I feel about that kind of talk."

He didn't even try to look contrite. "Yeah, yeah. You religious types."

"Troy. . ."

Troy put on his most charming smile and winked. Cindy knew other women frequently fell prey to Troy's good looks, wavy blond hair, blue eyes, and rascally smile, but his charms were all lost on her. They'd come too far in their friendship for that, but she was flattered that he still tried. As a concerned friend, her fondest wish was that, someday, he would give in to her frequent invitations to church and go with her.

Cindy grabbed the bill and stood. "Quit it. We're going to be late." Because she'd forgotten until the last minute, they had to take separate cars. Troy followed her there, and upon their arrival, Jacques, the leader, approached them.

"Oh, Cindy!" he exclaimed in his thick French accent. "My, but he is a big one, no?"

Cindy grinned. Since she was five-foot-nine, Troy, at six-foot-three, was one of the few men she could go out with and actually wear fashionable shoes.

"Follow me, please." Jacques waved Troy toward to the preparation area, and both men disappeared.

Jacques soon returned to explain the evening's scenario. Tonight, a man had fallen over a cliff in a climbing accident.

On the stage, Troy lay "unconscious" among some large stones. "Blood" spattered around him and a large "boulder" pinned his legs. Cindy wondered where Jacques borrowed the lovely huge fake rocks.

Troy would have done better if he hadn't been so ticklish, but he still made a good victim. After checking his vital signs, the team soon had him securely splinted and supported and all "bleeding" stopped. Then, they bound him into the stretcher, ready for the helicopter to take him away. The exercise ended when they "signaled" the helicopter to pull him up.

"Will I live?" Troy asked, still tied into the stretcher on the floor.

Cindy bent to pat him on the head. "Yes. And we're going to win the competition this year, all because of you."

Everyone applauded Troy for being such a good sport, Cindy untied him, then the group discussed the techniques they had used, and they were done.

Troy checked his watch. "I thought this would take longer. The night is still young. And I could sure use a coffee."

Cindy glanced toward Jacques, who had already begun to clean up. "You're so subtle, Troy. I have to stay a few minutes and talk to Jacques, but Erin will be home. I once talked her into being our victim, so I know you'll have something in common. Why don't you go on to my house? I won't be long."

Troy placed his hand over his heart, his fingers splayed. "I never turn down an invitation from a pretty woman." He waggled his eyebrows, but Cindy ignored him.

She helped Jacques with the last of the cleanup as she asked her questions, then she hurried out the door twenty minutes behind Troy, much later than she had intended.

To make matters worse, she found herself directly behind a slow-moving pickup truck hauling a bundle of oversized poles. No red warning flags dangled from the pipe ends, which protruded well beyond the rusty bumper. Only one single rope tied the bundle down. She didn't like being behind such a hazard, but traffic wouldn't allow her to skirt around the truck.

She was about to turn off on one of the side streets when the last car passed, allowing her to finally change lanes, only to find herself having to stop for the red light.

While she waited, a small, expensive-looking yellow sports car pulled up beside her, taking her place directly behind the idiot with the poles. The car's glossy paint shone, even in the dark. She harumphed to herself, thinking about how much such a car would be worth, which was likely at least the cost of her old duplex and then some.

The light changed, and the car in front of her started to proceed. She had just begun to inch forward when an earth-shattering crash assaulted her eardrums. Her car shook with the force of the nearby impact. The groan of bending metal and the smashing of breaking glass accompanied the sudden bang.

Cindy's stomach lurched as she gripped the steering wheel tight. It was beside her.

Flying debris bounced off the hood of her car as the noise from the impact reverberated in her brain. A large, older model car had rear-ended the sports car beside her, squashing it like an accordion into the truck ahead. The poles had broken through the windshield and protruded into the car.

First, Cindy said a quick prayer for the occupants, and after that, she didn't think. Ignoring the running motor, she yanked on the parking brake, grabbed her bag, and bolted to the yellow car. A lone man lay pinned inside, badly injured.

The mangled door refused to open, so Cindy kicked off her shoes, swept the broken glass off the crumpled hood, and squeezed into the space to lay half in and half out of the opening where the windshield had once been.

As she stared at the scene in front of her, nausea threatened to overwhelm her. With so much blood, she thought at first that the driver couldn't have possibly survived the impact, but she could see his chest moving, ever so slightly. His eyes were closed and his face contorted in pain. Still, he was alive. For now.

She quickly scanned him. Fortunately none of the poles impaled his body, but a couple of them had gouged the side of his chest, causing him to bleed profusely.

One of the poles had smashed his upper arm, and the steering wheel pressed tight against his body, presenting a high probability of internal injuries. His legs were pinned in the crushed vehicle, prohibiting Cindy from seeing them, but because of the car's angle, she strongly suspected that his left leg was broken.

Cindy reached to his neck to feel his pulse, but hesitated. "Can you hear me? I have my industrial first aid ticket, and I'm going to see what I can do for you until an ambulance gets here. Can you respond?"

He opened his mouth, but no sound came out. He tried to nod.

"That's okay. Don't move. Save your strength. From now on, just listen. And open your eyes so I know you're conscious."

His eyes, unfocused and glazed with pain, fluttered open.

"First I'm going to secure your arm. This is going to hurt, but I have to stop the bleeding. Please try and stay awake for me."

A mobile phone attached to the dash hung by the spiral cord. She wiggled farther into the squashed compartment to reach the handset. Trying not to bump the injured man and cause him any more pain, she planted herself almost on top of him.

Resting on her stomach with her legs sticking through where the windshield should have been, she dialed 911. She quickly told them what happened, requested the rescue squad with the Jaws of Life, and left the phone dangling, knowing the emergency staff would want to monitor the situation.

Frantically, Cindy rummaged through her first-aid bag, but she couldn't find the right piece to wrap the man's arm. She squeezed her eyes shut for a brief second, remembering it had been used on Troy for practice. Since she had to act fast, she pulled the scissors out of her bag and cut a jagged piece off her skirt, then wrapped his arm tightly. She tried to ignore the agony in the man's face and the deep moan that escaped through his clenched teeth.

People started to arrive, surrounding the car.

"You!" she called to a pale young man who looked as if he were about to be sick, "that's my car over there with the door open. Park it and come back with my keys."

She ignored everything else and gave her undivided attention to the injured man. In the middle of winter, all he wore was a very short pair of old cutoff jeans. But, she thanked God for his lack of proper seasonal attire, because now she could quickly assess the extent of his injuries without having to worry about clothing.

She searched his face. He didn't appear to have suffered any blows to the head. At least he had been wearing his seat belt. For a split second, it registered that he was about her age. Even through the suffering in his face, she could see his handsome features.

"Listen to me. I'm going to check you now. I have to see if there's anything I can do to help you. Keep listening, and keep your eyes open."

She could see he was trying to focus on her but couldn't.

"I'm going to run my hands down your legs. Try and keep still and tell me where it hurts."

She wiggled inside the mangled passenger compartment as best she could, squeezing in through the remaining narrow opening until she was fully inside. She ran her hands down his legs, trying not to be self-conscious as her fingers pushed through the coarse hair on her search for injuries that she could do something about. When her hand was past where she could see, she felt more blood, hot and wet, and sticky. His body jerked.

"Your leg is broken, and it's bad, but there's nothing I can do. I have no room to work here. Your legs are pinned. I can't move you."

Cindy next examined where the pole had imbedded in the car seat and pierced his side. She expected broken ribs, plus internal injuries, but her biggest concern was the heavy bleeding. Fortunately, he was able to breathe with his chest pinned tightly against the steering wheel.

"I'm going to have to use my hands to try to slow the bleeding. I'm going to apply pressure, and I can guarantee this will hurt. But if it makes you feel any better, my hands are clean," she said brightly, trying to distract him from what she knew was about to happen.

She grabbed a wad of rolled gauze from her bag. When she looked up into his face for a second, she thought he almost smiled at her little comment, but as she started to apply sufficient pressure, his expression jolted to extreme agony. His eyes squeezed shut and he clenched his teeth tightly.

"Look at me, please!" She had to keep him conscious and keep him from going into shock. With such injuries, shock was most likely to be followed by death.

His head sagged back against the seat, but his eyes were open, if only halfway. She could tell he was about to pass out. "Stay with me. Please. . ."

The movement of something touching her made Cindy jump. He had moved his arm, and his fingers brushed her hip.

Terrified that he was going to die, she changed her position until she could press his wound with only one hand. With the other blood-covered hand, she squeezed his outstretched hand, which had fallen after his feeble attempt to touch her. She thought she felt a faint return squeeze.

She examined his face. "You're going to make it," she croaked hoarsely. "I know you're going to make it." Cindy squeezed her eyes shut. She prayed he was going to make it. Clearing her throat and trying to focus her thoughts, she knew she had to continue talking so he would try harder to stay conscious. She started to babble, saying whatever came into her mind in order to help him focus his attention on anything but his agony.

By the time she heard the ambulance and detected the flashing red lights in the distance, she wasn't even aware of what she was saying.

Finally, a head appeared through the opening of what used to be the windshield as one of the rescue squad surveyed her and the nameless young man. "Keep applying pressure. We're going to have to cut him out."

"Affirmative," she replied, grateful that she could now take instructions from the experts. Looking at the young man, she saw his eyes starting to close. "Open your eyes. Only a few minutes longer. You did it! Come on, stay with me!" Cindy squeezed his fingers.

Between the Jaws of Life and the creaking sound of strained metal, she knew he'd never hear her over all the noise, so she quit trying to talk. The young man's eyes drifted shut, his entire body went limp, and he passed out. Cindy did the only thing she could. She prayed over him.

Dear God, please, I beg You to save this man. Please give him strength, courage, and the will to carry on. Please, use Your divine power to save his life, to heal him, and carry him through this. I pray for wisdom and skill for the hospital staff, the doctors, the nurses. Please spare his life. I pray Your never-ending mercy upon him. Amen.

Cindy's eyes sprang open as the car door was yanked off the hinges. Following procedure, the medical team applied a C-spine collar around his neck to hold his head steady and started an IV. The steering wheel began to lift, easing the pressure off his chest.

A hydraulic jack was inserted and lifted the wreckage off his legs. At last, he was free.

"All together, on three. Lady, keep up the pressure. One. Two. Three."

She awkwardly disengaged herself from the wreckage and stumbled along, trying to maintain enough pressure as they lifted his limp and broken body out of the car and onto a waiting stretcher. One of the attendants changed positions with her, finally leaving her hands unoccupied. Quickly, they lifted the stretcher into the waiting ambulance, the doors closed, and the ambulance roared off into the dark night, siren blaring and red lights flashing.

Cindy backed away from the wreckage. Every muscle in her body began to protest as the time spent in the awkward position inside the cramped car caught up with her. Across the street, police gave the driver of the older-model car a few basic roadside sobriety tests, then handcuffed him. The tow truck driver and another man, presumably the driver of the pickup truck, cleared the scattered poles and machinery parts.

Her hands started to shake as she bent to recover her shoes that she'd kicked off earlier. All the gory movies she'd seen in class had not adequately prepared her for this. Even with all her first aid training, she couldn't imagine facing what she had just been through without the unexpected strength and presence of mind that God had given her.

Fortunately, no one had come to talk to her yet. Her knees started to wobble so badly, she didn't know if she could stand much longer, so she ran to the smashed-up car, retrieved her scattered first-aid supplies, ran back to her own car, and drove away.

She had no idea how she got home or how long she took to

get there. Both her mind and body were numb. After parking the car, she leaned against the door for a few seconds before she touched the doorknob.

The second she entered, both Troy and Erin jumped to their feet.

"Cindy!" Erin called out. "Where were you? We were worried sick. You. . ."

She stood, frozen, staring back at them as they stared at her, first at her face, then her blood-splattered clothes. In the back of her mind, she wondered how much of her leg was showing since she ripped her skirt, but she really didn't care. Troy stepped forward but halted when she sagged backward against the wall.

"Cindy?!" Erin squeaked out from behind him. "What happened?"

Cindy dropped her purse and first-aid bag to the floor and hugged herself with both arms as she tried to piece everything together. "There was an accident beside me on the way home. The driver was badly hurt. And. . . And. . ." She gulped for breath as the backs of her eyes started to burn and her lower lip started to quiver. She felt the shock starting to take effect, but even knowing what was happening, she couldn't stop. Her voice caught, trembling as she spoke. "I don't think he's going to pull through."

Tears burst in a river down her cheeks. In a flash, Troy circled his arms around her as she started to sob, holding her tight and stroking her back as she cried herself out.

"Shhh," he whispered. "I know you did your best, more than anyone else could have done. You always say God has a reason for everything. I think He put you there to give him a better chance."

For a moment, she stilled. "Do you really think so?"

He gently tipped up her chin. "Tell you what," he said softly. "Let's phone the hospital. If you tell them you helped at the scene, they'll probably tell you his status."

Cindy glanced up at Troy and swiped her eyes with her

sleeve. "I'm sorry for getting so hysterical. I've never seen the man before in my life, yet I feel like I've lost a friend." She sniffled and blew her nose while Erin looked up the hospital's phone number.

Wanting to make the call in private, Cindy left Troy and Erin in the living room and made the call from her bedroom using her cell phone.

She returned to the living room as soon as she finished her call. "He's in surgery right now, and they won't have word on his prognosis until he's out—which they say may not be till morning. But, I'm glad to know he made it at least this far."

Troy stood and hugged Cindy again. "I'm really proud of you. It's not everyone who would jump in like that to help a stranger."

Cindy leaned into him. "I couldn't live with myself if I stood aside and did nothing while someone died for lack of attention." Her lower lip started to quiver again. "My parents died like that." She drew a shuddering breath, then turned away. "If you don't mind, I think I'm going to have a bath and go to bed."

"And I think it's time for me to leave." Troy smiled, nodded, gave her a gentle pat on the shoulder, and left.

While Cindy readied herself for bed, her thoughts returned to the scene of the accident. As she had so often heard, the drunk driver who caused the accident appeared not to have sustained any injuries. She'd seen him walking around, staggering.

She wondered about the injured man. Did he have a wife and children who would be worrying about him? If he lived, and she prayed he would, did he have friends who would visit him in the hospital in what would surely be a long recovery? Would he still be able to do his job, or would his injuries change his life forever? Cindy struggled not to cry again.

When she crawled into bed, she prayed intently, first pleading for the recovery of the accident victim's life, and next, giving thanks for her first aid training. She fell into an exhausted sleep and dreamed of a nameless young man in a crumpled yellow sports car.

two

Cindy awoke feeling like she had just run a marathon. Overnight, she had relived the accident scene a hundred times, interspersed with nightmares that hadn't reoccurred since childhood.

Since she had slept in, she phoned the hospital from her car on the way to work. The nurse wasn't supposed to give out details, but Cindy managed to find out that he'd been in surgery all night, he had not yet regained consciousness, and his condition was regarded as serious.

Cindy couldn't tell if his prognosis was good, but she left a message to tell him that God loved him, and then she prayed for him the rest of the way to work.

Troy was waiting for the elevator down as she was waiting for one going up. He wanted to talk, but as the door opened, she quickly assured him she was fine, then she ran into the elevator. All the way up to her office floor, she thought of how Troy, an alleged nonbeliever, had suggested it was God's intervention for her to be in the right place last night. By helping someone she would never see again, she had ministered to Troy.

Cindy quickly grabbed a coffee and delved into Robert's newest collection of correspondence and other assorted duties for the day. She hadn't been working for five minutes when Robert barked at her through the intercom, "I need a coffee. Bad."

She doubted her job description included the duty of waitress and she often told Robert so. However, she had recently badgered Robert into giving up cigarettes and he hadn't yet managed to control his irritation, not that he normally did, anyway. Over the past month, she learned that once she managed to get beyond Robert's rough exterior, he wasn't as bad to work with as everyone thought.

Instead of taking her chances by putting the steaming cup on the desk among the flow charts, contracts, proposals, and other assorted papers littering Robert's desk, Cindy handed the cup to him. She would never forget what happened on the first day on the job when Robert had spilled his coffee all over everything she'd struggled to get done. She'd been so overwhelmed by everything, in addition to being irritated by Robert's miserable disposition, that she'd lost control and snapped at him. Cindy Martins, a temporary replacement from the assembly line, proceeded to lecture the senior vice president on bad manners and being more careful.

Nothing was said, but she was positive her first day would also be her last. However, when she reported for work the next day, Robert greeted her with a smile on his face and a heavy-duty ceramic coffee mug in his hand. She still didn't understand, but she wasn't going to argue.

"Do you need anything else?"

He grunted, but smiled for a second when Cindy grunted back, although he still didn't take her not-so-subtle hint about grunting in the first place.

Cindy returned to her desk and continued her work and thought about the recent changes in her life. Somehow, despite her inexperience and all her mistakes in dealing with Robert—both on a personal and professional level, she managed to earn his respect and deal with the workload. After her first week on the job, she had nearly fainted when Robert not only offered her the job on a permanent basis but also offered to double her salary if she would stay. Of course she accepted. God had met her needs—and then some.

First, she went out and bought more clothes. Up until that point, she only owned a couple of good mix-and-match outfits she wore to church, which she'd sewn herself to save money. After her first shopping spree, she decided to put some money aside each payday into an education fund. In the fall, she wanted to enroll in a college night course and improve her business skills without having to take out a student loan. The increase in her pay also meant she could live on something better than macaroni and wieners.

The phone rang. "Mr. Blackmore's office."

A male voice spoke roughly. "I need to speak to Robby."

Cindy pulled out her notepad. "I'm sorry, *Mr. Blackmore* is tied up. Would you care to leave a message?"

His voice dropped to an annoyed growl. "I know he's there. I want to talk to him."

She recalled Robert's latest gruntfest. "I'm sorry, he's unable to take your call. Is there a message?"

"I don't have time to leave a message. I want to talk to him."

Cindy held her breath to control herself, suspecting that this man had learned his manners from the same place as her boss. Both of them needed a refresher course.

Her voice lowered and, trying to remember to be polite, she ground out her response between clenched teeth. "I'm very sorry, but I have to take a message."

"This is Glen Evans. I want to talk to him."

Cindy held the phone away from her face, stuck out her tongue, and then balanced the phone on her shoulder while she reached for her pen. "Let me see. Hmmm. . .Glen Evans," she drawled, writing his name down very slowly, mumbling every letter singly so he could hear she was taking her time in payback for his rudeness. "And your phone number, please?"

Glen Evans sighed loudly. "He has my number."

She knew the state of Robert's address book. "I'd prefer to write it down."

A loud laugh echoed on the other end of the line. "You must be the new secretary. 555-2974."

Cindy wrote the number quickly, mumbled a good-bye, and whacked the button sharply with her finger to disconnect, although it would have felt much better to slam the receiver down in his ear.

The light clicking of the other secretaries' computers was noticeably absent. Cindy raised her head to see that none of them were working and all of them were staring at her.

"What?" she snapped.

"Glen Evans?" Ann gulped. "You spoke like that to Glen Evans?"

Cindy dragged her free hand over her face. "Why do I have the feeling I've done something really wrong?"

"You've got guts," Melinda said, shaking her head. "No one else could ever get away with something like that—or half the things you do. How do you get away with it?"

She shrugged her shoulders, then ripped the message off the notepad. "Just lucky, I guess." Every day as a secretary for Robert Blackmore was an adventure. Although Cindy wished that she could learn some of these lessons the easy way.

⁂

Cindy cringed as she noted the date circled on her desk calendar. Officially six months since she started her new job, today was the day of her salary and performance review. Today, Robert Blackmore would see her personnel file. Up until now, Troy had taken the liberty of "accidentally" losing it every time Robert asked for it. Thus far, they had gotten away with the ploy.

Robert called her in to his office as she returned from her coffee break, preventing her from making any excuses. He sat behind his large desk, leaning back in his oversized chair with his arms crossed over his belly.

He pushed a piece of paper across the desk. "I'd like you to read this before I comment."

Cindy swallowed hard, gathering the courage she needed. Surprisingly, all the expected categories of general performance skills were checked as "very good" or "excellent." Under the "general comments" he had written such a glowing report that she actually blushed.

When she raised her head, he leaned forward and folded his hands on the desk. Cindy held her breath and stared at the floor. "Thank you," she mumbled. "I don't know what to say."

"Let me be candid with you." Robert cleared his throat and

his voice deepened in pitch as he continued. "When you first got here, I thought you were someone's best attempt at getting back at me for something."

She couldn't help it. She hunched her shoulders and shrank back in her chair. She would never forget her conversation with Troy the day the position came open or his attitude toward Robert, which had not improved. Because of the confidential nature of her position, the only thing she could tell Troy was that she and Robert had developed a mutual respect for each other. Until that happened, she'd spent many nights deep in prayer, begging God for strength, patience, peace of mind, and whatever it took to get the job done. She had real proof that God answered prayers.

Finally, he continued. "You had no respect for my authority, and you had no idea what you were doing. Don't think I couldn't tell." He grinned, and she forced herself to smile back. "The only reason I kept you on that week was because I was desperate. And then, by Friday, I saw that, due to your organizational skills, I was actually making progress again."

Not sure if she had been complimented or not, Cindy blinked and stared.

"After awhile, I found myself enjoying my job again. I even quit smoking, and you kept my dander up enough to make me want to stick with it."

Robert paused again, as if waiting for her to comment. Cindy sat, speechless.

"Before we discussed your raise I wanted to see your personnel file, but every time I ask Troy Thompson for it, he makes some excuse. Tell me, who lost out and what were you doing before we hired you as a diamond in the rough."

Cindy stiffened her posture in the chair and folded her hands in her lap. She briefly sucked on her lower lip, then stared him straight in the eyes. "I worked for Fred's Automotive Supplies," she said abruptly.

His brows knotted, probably trying to figure out why old Fred would have needed a secretary.

"I was the shipper/receiver," she blurted out. "And forklift operator."

Troy had warned her that Robert would never stand for the gibes that would surely follow after everyone found out that his secretary turned out to be a lowly warehouse man, or warehouse woman as the guys had called her. And he would never forgive her for making him look like a fool, however unintentional. While Robert couldn't outright fire her, Troy warned her that very soon he'd make her want to quit.

She hadn't meant to deceive Robert, they'd just never gotten around to talking about her past experience. Robert wasn't stupid. He obviously knew she hadn't had the experience to go with the job when she first started. However, she knew he wouldn't have expected this.

"Forklift operator?" The corners of his mouth started to curl upward as he stared at her. She could almost feel his gaze as he studied her from head to foot, taking in her dress, color-coordinated panty hose, matching high-heeled shoes, and new hairstyle, a far cry from the coveralls and safety work boots she wore in the parts warehouse.

He didn't break eye contact the entire time. "Shipper/receiver?" he asked again.

Unable to believe her eyes, Cindy watched as Robert leaned back in his chair, threw his head back, and laughed so hard his belly shook. She wondered if the entire floor could hear his loud guffaws, even with the door closed. Tears streamed from his eyes, which he wiped as his laughter started to subside.

"Oh, that's good," he chuckled. "That's really good. I haven't laughed like that in years. What a deadpan delivery. You really had me going there for awhile. I don't think I've ever heard you crack a joke before."

He laughed softly again. "I don't know what's with you and Thompson, but one day I'll find out. I'm going to give you a ten percent raise."

Cindy waffled between feeling relieved, insulted, and ecstatic at the raise. She mumbled a thank-you and headed for the coffee machine instead of her desk.

"Bring me one, too!" Robert called out after her. She heard him chuckle again. "I think I need it."

Her hands shook as she poured both cups of coffee. As funny as Robert thought she was, she had told the truth. Her first job out of high school was delivering parts for Fred. As his clientele grew and he needed to expand—after a lot of convincing that a woman could do it—he gave her the shipper/receiver position. She'd enjoyed the job, until Fred retired and his son shut the company down and took off with the money. Most of all, she had appreciated the informal atmosphere working with the mechanics, truck drivers, and a few of Fred's more eccentric clients, which was quite different than working with the executive and secretarial staff at Circuits, Inc.

Senior Vice President Robert Blackmore was in a category unto himself.

After delivering Robert's coffee, she slunk away to her desk, where she worked in silence until lunch, then she tagged along with the other secretaries in order to keep her mind busy with meaningless small talk.

Upon their return, all five of them discovered mountains of paperwork invading their desks.

"What is this?" Brenda waved one arm over the onslaught of paper. "It's not year end."

Cindy, too, couldn't believe the unprecedented volume that appeared out of nowhere. Robert littered sticky notes on everything, labeling most of the work as "urgent." Resigned, she heaved a sigh and picked through the stacks of files and folders, knowing that the sooner she got to the work, the less overtime she would be forced to work.

To her dismay, in addition to the heavy workload, the phones rang nonstop. Trying to settle the phone on her shoulder, she searched frantically for the pen she had in her hand only a second ago. She was caught off guard when she looked forward, straight into the stomach of a well-dressed man in an expensive, European-cut suit.

When Cindy made eye contact with the visitor, she nearly dropped the phone. The man was significantly younger than the other businessmen who visited Robert, and a lot better looking, too. Since she was still on the phone, she nodded to acknowledge him.

Despite his age, which she guessed would only be a few years older than her own twenty-six, he carried a distinguished air about him, yet his smile radiated warmth rather than cool professionalism. His nearly black hair, which was longer on the top than the sides, had a light wave and framed his face to emphasize slightly rounded cheeks and a pair of gorgeous dimples. Even his nose, straight and patrician, was attractive.

Cindy collected herself and concentrated on the phone call.

When she hung up, the visitor handed her a business card. "My name is Montgomery Smythe. I have a two o'clock appointment with Robert Blackmore."

Cindy hit the intercom button, but spoke to Robert through the phone for privacy to tell him his appointment had arrived.

After hanging up the phone, she looked up at Mr. Smythe, who responded to her acknowledgment of him with a smile and a nod, indicating fine manners, unlike many of Robert's visitors, especially the notorious Glen Evans. She returned his smile and folded her hands on the desk in front of her. "I'm sorry, but Mr. Blackmore will be about fifteen minutes. Would you like to have a seat?"

As she spoke, his face paled and his eyes widened as though he had just seen a ghost. He stood still for a second, straightened his tie awkwardly, backed into the visitor's chair catty-cornered from her desk, and sank down, never taking his eyes off her.

Cindy stifled an urge to run to the washroom, worried she had ketchup or something equally embarrassing on her nose. She discreetly glanced down at her blouse, but all her buttons were fastened. Rather than get up, she quickly stole a peek at herself in the reflection of Robert's office window but couldn't see anything obviously wrong.

Continuing to work, she tried very hard not to let him get to her, but after a few minutes of knowing she was being watched, she couldn't stand it anymore. She met his eyes, but he didn't stop staring at her, even though she stared right back.

Fortunately, the phone rang again, providing her with a welcome distraction. With the phone tucked into her shoulder, she continued her conversation and turned to retrieve a file from the cabinet.

When she turned forward again, Mr. Smythe was standing beside her desk. He must have thought she was too busy to look at him because he was leaning toward her with his eyes closed, making no effort to hide the fact that he was inhaling her perfume.

Cindy gritted her teeth, reassessing her opinion of him.

His eyes opened, and he blatantly listened to her conversation the entire time she talked on the phone. When she hung up, she wanted to throw the phone at him. And her pen. And the file containing the customer's contracts, except that its contents were confidential.

She slammed the folder closed, then squeezed her eyes shut. Determined to remain professional, Cindy folded her hands in the center of her desk and forced herself to smile politely between clenched teeth. "Can I help you with something?"

He leaned slightly forward. Cindy leaned backward. "Do I look familiar to you?"

If she hadn't known better, he could have been the brother of Robert's notorious friend Glen Evans. They shared the same dark features, although this man's countenance was softer, and he was much better looking.

Since he stood so close, she looked into his eyes, which were the darkest chocolate brown she had ever seen, without a fleck of olive or green or any other color in them. They were gorgeous eyes. Eyes a woman could get lost in.

She blinked, ashamed of herself. "Not really. Do you have a brother?"

He shook his head and leaned closer. His voice held a slight waver that hadn't been there a minute ago. "No, I don't. Think back about five months."

That was about the time she'd started working for Robert, but she didn't remember seeing him before. She picked up his business card, which stated that he was Montgomery Edward Smythe, the systems manager from Smythe Computer Systems. Before working for Robert she had never dealt with any kind of manager, nor did she know anyone who even had a management job.

She tried to think of something away from work. They couldn't possibly shop at the same supermarket because she lived in a dumpy neighborhood, and his suit was probably worth more than her car. The last place she thought of was church, but she knew everyone in the small congregation, at least by face, having attended there since she was a child. Besides, he appeared to be the type of man who couldn't be forgotten.

Cindy looked at him as he continued to watch her. Her mind raced as she fought for a clue, anything that would jog her memory. She tried to make eye contact with any of the other secretaries for a hint, but they were too busy staring at him as he stared at her.

He rested his palms flat on her desktop, and out of the corner of her eye, she noticed that his hands were shaking. "Think. Where have you seen me before?"

She honestly couldn't place him, but he apparently recognized her from somewhere, although it wasn't enough to say from where it was. Either that or he was playing some kind of game with her. Cindy was not amused.

"I don't know," she stammered, knowing everyone was watching. She felt nervous enough without an audience. "Have you ever driven a truck for a living?" She doubted he worked as one of the mechanics on her delivery route from her early days with Fred, but anything was possible, and at this point, she felt desperate.

"No, but I did drive a yellow Porsche."

"A Porsche?" She didn't know anyone with that kind of money. In the back of her mind, she tried to remember what a Porsche looked like. Then her brain nearly went into overdrive as she stared into his face. The perfectly straight nose, the very dark hair—those and other small details started falling into place.

Cindy gasped out loud and covered her mouth with both hands. "You!" she gulped. "In the little yellow sports car!"

The man's posture stiffened as he ran one hand over his hair, then rammed both hands into his pockets. His voice came out in a hoarse croak. "I wasn't absolutely positive until now, but it was you. You didn't tell me your name."

Cindy couldn't help but stare, taking in every inch of him from head to foot. That night in the car she had been too busy to study him closely, but what she'd seen had not been pleasant. The dark of nighttime had not hidden the blood splattered everywhere and the horror of his life-threatening injuries. Despite his tousled hair hanging in his face that night, she would never forget the agony in his expression and the hopelessness of what little movement he'd been able to do while he was trapped, waiting for what felt like an eternity.

Now in the bright light of the office she could see him perfectly, and he was a sight to behold. His immaculate and perfectly fitted, custom-tailored suit shouted style and money, and most of all, confidence. Everything about him was perfect, even his hair, which was combed and gelled back into a neat, executive style.

"I didn't recognize you. You're. . ." She paused for the right word to describe the difference. Words failed her. ". . .okay."

"I recognized your voice and your perfume." He fumbled in his breast pocket and put on a pair glasses, then leaned over her desk until his face was about a foot and a half from hers. Already leaning as far back in her chair as possible, Cindy couldn't move away. "I'm very farsighted. I didn't see your face, especially since you were so close. I tried to find out who you were, but you disappeared without a trace. I have to see you again."

"No!" She shook her head violently.

He returned the glasses to his pocket and straightened. "Please, let me take you out for dinner or something, so we can talk."

Cindy hugged the file folder in front of her, using it as a barrier. "No, I can't."

"I know there's nothing I can do to ever repay you, but please let me do something. At least let me replace the dress you wore that night."

"That's really not n-necessary. . . ."

"Please."

"No, I don't want anything from you. . . ."

"I don't even know your name."

"Cindy," she choked out. "My name is Cindy."

The intercom buzzed, and Robert's voice blared through it. "You can send him in now."

Cindy stared at him in silence. Visibly shaken, he stared back. "You'd better go in now," she said unsteadily.

He stiffened his posture. "Yes, of course."

And Montgomery Smythe walked into Robert's office.

Cindy couldn't help but notice his limp.

The door closed, but she couldn't look away. For the longest time, he had haunted her dreams. Now the man had a name.

She forced herself to open the file in the middle of her desk, but her brain didn't register a single word. She could only raise her head to stare sightlessly at Robert's closed door.

"Cindy? Are you okay?"

"What happened?"

"Who is that man?"

Cindy blinked and turned. All four secretaries stared at her. "What?" She cleared her throat.

"Are you okay? What did he say about replacing your clothes? Has he done something to hurt you?"

"No," Cindy mumbled. "Nothing like that."

They continued to stare at her. Cindy lowered her head and pretended to concentrate on her work, never wanting a day to end so quickly.

three

"Good afternoon, Mr. Smythe. I'm pleased to finally meet you. Have a seat."

Monty returned Robert Blackmore's handshake and sat in the chair in front of the large desk, trying to regain his composure. He stared into the man's face, but his mind was blank. He only saw the face of the man's secretary. Her name was Cindy.

As much as he tried, he couldn't concentrate, even after months of planning and dozens of grueling hours of preliminary work. He started planning his presentation while laid up in the hospital.

Trapped was more like it. Lying immobile in a hospital bed for weeks, then stuck at home, incapacitated for eons. His long, drawn-out recovery had almost driven him crazy.

Much of that time, he'd thought about his special angel. Of course he knew she wasn't a real angel, but in those weeks following the accident, in his mind, she was. He'd woken up a week after the accident in a fog. Then, he'd drifted in and out of consciousness for a few more days until he managed to stay awake with the biggest headache of his life. In addition to his head, his whole body ached in different ways, parts of which still hurt, even after all this time.

He never saw her face clearly. Not only had it been dark, but without his glasses, he couldn't make out any details closer than an arm's length in front of his face. In the tight quarters of his squashed car, she had been practically on top of him. His agonizing pain hadn't improved his focus either. He couldn't see anything clearly after the collision at any distance. He'd never been in such pain in his life and hoped never to be again.

And just when he thought he was going to die, he heard her talking to God.

When he was finally coherent enough to speak and let everything sink in, the surgeon told him that, had it not been for the woman who appeared at the scene of the accident, he would have bled to death. In addition, if she hadn't requested the right equipment to free him immediately from the wreckage, he would have died from the delay. The surgeons thought they'd lost him twice during surgery. It had been close.

He had no idea who she was. No one did. When he was finally able to get around, he'd tried to find her, although he still hadn't figured out how he could ever express proper thanks for what she had done. He eventually tracked down everyone who'd seen her. Everyone. The police said she disappeared before they could take a statement. They didn't even know what kind of car she drove. The ambulance attendants said she used a piece of her clothing to control some of the bleeding. The rescue squad said she did all the right things. The hospital staff said she'd phoned twice but only left the short message that God loved him and didn't leave her name. Apparently, she'd called both times from a cell phone, because the hospital had no record of the number she'd called from. In desperation, he even talked to the tow truck driver, but he didn't remember seeing her.

As a last resort, he managed to pin down the person who spoke to her at 911. They couldn't trace her with the phone call, either. She'd called from his own car phone. They finally got so sick of hearing from him that they gave him a copy of the tape of the conversation. He couldn't count the number of times he'd listened to it. The tape provided was the only tangible proof he had of her existence. He would never forget that soft melodic voice until his dying day—which, thanks to her, hadn't been that night five months ago.

Just when he'd given up all hope of finding her, here she was. Now he'd seen her clearly, in the light. She had ordinary dark brown hair and a rather big nose for a woman. She wasn't particularly pretty, but up close she had the most compelling smoky gray eyes. She exuded an inner strength that showed clearly, even on this, their first real meeting.

He'd finally met her face-to-face. He was stunned.

And her perfume. He had no idea why such a thing would stick in his mind, but one day in the mall he'd nearly had a heart attack when he smelled the same perfume while walking past the cosmetic counter. He didn't know why he did it, but he bought a bottle. The brand wasn't even expensive stuff. It still sat on the vanity in his washroom as a reminder every day. As if he needed one. Being able to wake up in the morning was reminder enough.

And here she was. The voice. The perfume. Her name was Cindy.

"Are you all right, Mr. Smythe?" The senior vice president's voice brought Monty back to the present.

He cleared his throat and adjusted his tie to bide himself some time until his hands stopped shaking. "Yes." He nodded, then shook his head. The entire presentation he'd worked on for months disappeared in the blink of an eye. "No, I'm not. I'm sorry, Mr. Blackmore. I apologize for the inconvenience, but I have to talk to your secretary."

"My secretary? What for?"

Monty faced Mr. Blackmore, knowing he could possibly blow the most lucrative contract of his career. "I have to talk to her. She saved my life and disappeared. I've been looking for her for months, and I can't let her get away again."

"She saved your life? Cindy? My Cindy? How?"

His gut clenched just thinking about it. After talking to so many people, he'd put all the pieces together about what happened and who did what. The only thing he hadn't been able to find was the missing mystery woman. "About five months ago I was in a very serious automobile accident. She appeared out of nowhere, administered some life-saving first aid, and disappeared without telling anyone her name. I'm sorry, but my mind has just gone blank. I'd like to reschedule another appointment. And please accept my apologies."

Robert turned his head in Cindy's direction, as did Monty, to watch the shadow of her form through the curtained window. "Were you really hurt that bad?"

Monty nodded. "It was touch-and-go for awhile. Without her, they say I would have died."

"Wow."

Monty tried not to squirm as Robert scanned him from head to foot. "And you're all right now?"

"Except for a quantity of metal holding me together and a number of assorted scars, I'm fine." He stood.

"Sure, book another appointment with my secretary." Robert paused, grinned as he glanced again through the curtain, then walked around his desk to open the door. "I've enjoyed our conversation today, Mr. Smythe. And please call me Robert. I look forward to meeting with you again."

"Thank you, Robert." Monty returned the handshake. "And please, call me Montgomery."

Monty headed straight for Cindy's desk, where she sat with her head bowed, concentrating intently on her work. She stopped typing as soon as she realized he was there.

"I'd like to book another appointment with Robert, but I'll have to do that when I get back to my office." He cleared his throat and wiggled the knot of his tie for lack of something better to do with his hands. His tie had never been so straight. "And I really would like to see you again, somewhere private, so we can talk."

Her face flushed. "It's okay," she whispered, glancing from side to side before making eye contact. "Don't worry about it."

"But I want to. I have so much I want to say to you. Is there anything I can do for you?"

"I don't want anything from you. Really. If you want to do something, why don't you just send me a few flowers, and that'll be enough."

"Flowers? That's it?"

"Yes." Her voice dropped. "Just a few flowers. I like fresh flowers."

"Flowers it is." Monty reached out, grasped her hand, and bending forward, brought it up to his lips and kissed it, something he'd never done in his life, but the action felt strangely right. "I'm glad I finally got to meet you. Good-bye, Cindy."

He released her hand, bowed, turned, and trying his best to minimize his limp, walked into the elevator and out to his car.

❧

Cindy watched Montgomery Edward Smythe disappear as the elevator door closed, her mind still reeling from the events of the day.

First, her performance review, which she didn't want to think about, and now this.

"Wow," Ann sighed.

"Yeah. Wow," Brenda sighed, too.

Susan rested her elbows on her desk and cradled her chin in her cupped palms. "Who is he, and why didn't you tell us about him?"

"Why can't he buy *me* flowers?" Melinda giggled.

"There's nothing to tell. I don't even know him," Cindy stammered. The only ones that knew about what had happened were Troy and Erin. And she planned to keep it that way. "He needed some help one day, and I was there."

Out of the corner of her eye, Cindy noticed Robert standing in the doorway of his office listening to the conversation. "You're lying, Cindy." Robert's voice echoed in the hushed room.

All the women turned to see his rotund figure leaning against the door frame. Cindy shrank in her chair, wishing the ground would swallow her up.

"Well, maybe not lying, but that certainly isn't the entire truth. He told me what happened. In fact, he was so shaken up after meeting you, he couldn't concentrate, so we had to make another appointment."

All eyes turned to Cindy, followed by an audible gasp.

Cindy's face heated up, and she nearly dropped the file she had been preparing.

"In fact," Robert continued, undaunted, "I think I'm going to tell you all what really happened. Come on, Cindy, don't be embarrassed." He faced the other ladies.

Cindy shrank farther down into her chair. She tried to continue working, but her hands shook too much.

"He was in a car accident, and Cindy did more than just help. He says she saved his life, then left without telling anyone who she was."

"Ooohhhhhh. . . ," all four ladies gushed, staring at her, making her wish for a cave nearby so she could go hide.

"Please," she begged, "don't tell anyone. It wasn't that big a deal. I just did what needed to be done."

"It was a big deal to him, Cindy," said Robert gravely. "But that is now between you and him, right, ladies?"

"Yes, Mr. Blackmore," they mumbled in unison.

"Want the rest of the day off, Cindy?" he asked.

Cindy wondered if Robert could see her shaking. "No, I'm really busy, and it's not like it happened yesterday or anything. But thanks for the offer."

The volume of paperwork helped get her back on track, and soon everyone was hard at work again, ignoring her, just the way she wanted it.

❧

After a restless night, Cindy arrived at her desk to find a dozen pink roses in a lovely crystal vase tied with a large white ribbon waiting for her. She read the card.

A few flowers won't ever come close to what I wanted to say, but they will have to do. Hope you enjoy them—
                                                    Montgomery

She smiled and ran her fingers along the velvety petals, then buried her face into the bouquet, inhaling the heady fragrance. Since the shock of seeing him was gone, she could appreciate his gesture. Montgomery was probably very nice.

After rummaging through her desk, she read the business card he had left the day before.

She wondered about the connection from his name to the company but then dismissed the thought. It was not her concern.

Card in hand, she dialed his number. When the receptionist put her call through, Cindy was surprised that he answered his own phone and not a secretary.

"Hello, Montgomery. This is Cindy Martins, from Circuits, Inc. I just wanted to call to thank you for the flowers. They're very nice, although I would hardly call a dozen roses a few flowers, but thank you."

"Please, call me Monty, and I'm glad you liked them. So tell me, what would you term 'a few' flowers then?"

She giggled. "Two or three. Just a few, not a dozen. To tell the truth, no one has ever given me a dozen roses before, and while you did make me feel rather special, they were too much, just the same. I thought I'd call and say thank you."

"You're more than welcome."

"I've got to get back to work now. Thanks again. Bye, Monty."

"Bye, Cindy."

With that out of the way, Cindy returned her attention to her work. As the day progressed, she developed a whopping headache, which she initially attributed to a poor night's sleep after the stress of the day before. However, by the end of the day, her monster headache had worsened to the extent that she wondered if her head would explode. Her sinuses were blocked solid, her nose started to run, and she couldn't stop shivering.

When she arrived home, Cindy dug through the medicine cabinet in search of some heavy-duty cold medication. Tonight she had planned to go out for dinner with Troy and then to the theater to see a play she had been looking forward to for weeks, and she refused to let a little cold stop her.

She pulled a spare blanket out of the closet to keep herself warm until the medication took effect, flopped down on the couch, and absently stared at the pink roses.

The next thing she knew, her head shot up at the sound of pounding on the door. She tried to move her hands to push herself up, but she was all tangled in the blanket.

Erin, whom she hadn't heard come home, answered the door.

Troy strode in. "Hi, how's it. . . You look terrible! Are you sick?"

Cindy sniffled. "Thanks, I needed that. I feel much better now." She sneezed.

Before she had the chance to stand, Troy frowned and pressed his hand on her forehead. "You're running a fever. How long have you felt like this? And where did you get the flowers?"

Cindy tried to smile, but her eyes burned. All she could do was squint upward at him. "I started feeling crummy at lunchtime. You remember that car accident the night you were our victim? The flowers are from him."

"That's it? He gave you flowers?"

"He wanted me to go out with him and talk, but I told him all I wanted was a few flowers, and he sent me a dozen roses. Wasn't that sweet?"

"Humph," Troy mumbled, scowling at the beautiful bouquet. "Yeah, sweet." He tucked the blanket around her chin, then stood back. "What about the play tonight?"

Suppressing a sniffle, Cindy tried to smile, but her attempt didn't work. Her nose was so stuffed she couldn't breathe, and on top of everything else, now her eyes were watery. Her head fell back on the couch and the blanket fell from where Troy had tucked it. She shivered.

"I'm fine." She pulled the blanket up again, and the movement brought on a fit of coughing.

"Right. You look fine. I think we can forget about dinner, too."

"Oh, Troy," she moaned. "I'm so sorry. I know you wanted to see the play. Why don't you and Erin go?" She sniffled, making her head hurt even worse.

Erin and Troy froze and stared at each other.

Cindy squeezed her eyes shut. "I'm not trying to be a matchmaker, but I don't want to waste the tickets." She sneezed again.

Suddenly, Troy grinned, showing off his wonderful smile and sparkling blue eyes. Cindy nearly started to admonish him that his charms were not going to work, but she started coughing.

Troy's smile dropped to a downcast expression and he let out an exaggerated sigh. His head fell back, he lifted the back of his hand to touch his forehead, and he laid his other palm over his heart, his fingers splayed. "Oh, Erin," he moaned melodramatically. "I've been stood up! Please help me salvage my broken heart!"

Erin groaned at his terrible theatrics. Cindy wanted to hit him.

He lowered himself to one knee before Erin, then grasped her left hand with his right. His eyes twinkled as he smiled engagingly at Erin, and her face flushed in return.

"Erin, would you honor me by being my guest to the theater tonight? I just happen to have great seats." He bowed his head with a dramatic flourish.

Erin giggled, then snatched her hand away. "I'll be dressed in ten minutes." She disappeared into her bedroom before Cindy could blink twice.

Cindy gritted her teeth at the thought of Erin falling for that rot. She glared at Troy. "How do you do that?"

Troy shrugged his shoulders. "I have a gift."

"She's my best friend. I'm warning you."

"Me?"

"Yes, you."

He tipped his head back and laughed aloud. Cindy ignored him and sagged back into the soft, comfy couch, which shifted when Troy sat to wait for Erin. Cindy felt herself dozing off again, but she didn't care. She never heard them leave.

Sometime in the middle of the night Cindy awoke, finding herself still on the couch with her trusty blanket. She made a much needed trip to the washroom and crawled off to bed.

In the morning, she didn't feel any better and phoned in sick. Not that she expected sympathy from her boss, but she couldn't tell if Robert was teasing when he reminded her about how his previous secretary phoned in sick, then quit. After thinking about it all day and all the following night, she went in the next day despite not being fully recovered.

She felt infinitely better when Robert nearly dropped his coffee cup as she walked by his office and sat down at her desk, which was piled high with folders and loose papers. She didn't know how so much could accumulate in one day.

Within seconds, Robert appeared beside her, the cup still in his hand. "What are you doing here?"

"I work here. Don't I?" She sneezed.

"I didn't expect you today. I guess you can tell I missed you. And by the way, Montgomery phoned for you yesterday. I left you a note."

He had stuck a note with Monty's name and phone number in the center of her computer screen, along with other notes concerning matters requiring her immediate attention.

"Did he say what he wanted?"

"Didn't ask. But I think it was important."

She also noticed his card wasn't in her drawer but sitting on top of the phone.

She called him right away. As soon as she identified herself, the receptionist put her through immediately. "Hi, Monty. It's Cindy, from Circuits, Inc., returning your call."

"It's great to hear from you. How are you feeling? Robert said you were sick yesterday."

"I'm not great, but I feel much better than I did yesterday. Thanks for asking. Now what can I do for you?"

"I need to make an appointment to see Robert."

Cindy raised her eyebrows. He could have made the

appointment himself by speaking with Robert. Neither of them needed her just for that.

She flipped through Robert's appointment book. "How does ten-thirty Friday morning sound?"

"Fine. I'll see you at the same time, too."

"Can't miss me, I sit right outside his office door, and you won't get in unless I say so."

He laughed. "I wish I had a secretary like you. Maybe someday. See you tomorrow. Bye."

Later that morning, more flowers arrived—a small but lovely arrangement of three fragrant blossoms she couldn't identify, surrounded by dainty baby's breath. The card was brief and to the point.

> *A few flowers, as requested.*
> *Monty*

Cindy frowned as she reread the card. She had not requested any more flowers. In fact, quite the opposite. She told him a dozen was too much and that. . . and that she only wanted a few flowers, like two or three.

Cindy grinned in spite of herself.

Throughout the day, her attention wandered to the vase of flowers on the corner of her desk. While she fought with the piles of paperwork, she continually tried to inhale their delicate fragrance as best she could through her stuffy nose. Every time she looked at them, she thought of Monty.

Her smile faded. That was probably his intention, and she wasn't falling for it.

All day long, she struggled to catch up with the backlog, and by the time she got home, she felt exhausted. Sitting on the couch, she was halfway falling asleep when Erin ran in the door and straight to her bedroom.

"Where are you going in such a rush?" she called out.

"I've got to change. Troy is going to be here in fifteen minutes, and we're going out for dinner."

Cindy nearly dropped the remote control. She headed to Erin's room to question her but found her in the washroom, frantically fixing her hair. "You're going out with Troy? That was quick. You just went out with him night before last."

"I went out with him last night, too, but you were sleeping and didn't notice," Erin mumbled as she applied her makeup.

Cindy crossed her arms. "You watch that man. He's got more lines than a high school notebook. I should know. He used every one of them on me."

Erin spoke while applying her lipstick. "You didn't fall for any of them, did you?"

Cindy grinned. "Well, no. I thought they were kind of cute." She giggled. "And he tries so hard. I think I bruised his ego when I told him I only wanted to be friends. You should see the women at work drooling over him."

"Don't worry about me." Erin winked. "I'm a big girl."

"But he's a big boy."

Erin winked. "Yeah, I know. Isn't he great?"

Cindy lost her smile. "Erin, he's an unbeliever. While I like him as a friend, I don't know if the relationship you have in mind with him is such a good idea."

"I know. But we've talked a lot about spiritual things, and he's really thinking about it. Trust me, okay? Like, I'm not going to run out and marry the guy. At least not yet."

Troy knocked at the door, and they nodded at each other as Erin opened it.

"Where are we going?" Erin asked as she slipped on her shoes. "Remember you're paying."

Troy only grinned and waved to Cindy as they exited.

After they disappeared out the door, Cindy took another dose of cold medication and crawled off to bed.

❧

Stepping out of the office elevator, Cindy immediately noticed a vase containing three flowers on her desk. This time the arrangement consisted of a red fascia, a yellow daisy mum, and a white carnation. Only two words appeared on the card.

"Guess who?" The riddle didn't take much guesswork to solve.

She set the flowers aside and immediately started working. Before long, Robert appeared beside her with more work.

"More flowers?"

Cindy mumbled her affirmation as she took the file from his hand and immediately started typing.

Robert stayed beside her. "He told me he wants to take you out to say thank you."

She made a typo and backspaced over it. "I know," she mumbled, trying to concentrate on the client's contract. "But, I told him just to send me a few flowers, so he did. I'm sure he'll soon forget about me."

"Maybe," Robert mumbled, studying the flowers. "Maybe not."

four

Another bouquet awaited her arrival. Today it was a red begonia, a yellow chrysanthemum, and a white lilac in a thin earthen vase. Lilacs were out of season, and she didn't even want to venture a guess as to how much this little enterprise was costing him. The card mentioned his appointment with Robert, which she noted was unfortunately scheduled just before another visit from the annoying Glen Evans.

She had collected a stack of magazines to keep Glen occupied, but she needed to talk to Monty.

Monty arrived early. He stood in front of her, smiling, not even acknowledging his gift of the flowers on the corner of her desk.

Cindy couldn't look away from his dark brown eyes. The beginning of laugh lines at their corners mesmerized her. She normally wouldn't have associated laugh lines with his stark professional image, yet they somehow strengthened it.

She folded her hands on her desk. "Thanks for the flowers. They're lovely, but I'd like you to stop sending them."

"I thought you said you liked flowers."

"Of course I like them, but you've sent so many that saying thank you doesn't seem like enough."

His smile widened, heightening the little laugh lines. Her breath caught. "I said once before that a few flowers would never say all that I wanted. How about going out to lunch with me so I can say everything I need to say? Would today work for you?"

She couldn't think with him looking at her like that, so she pretended to study the flowers while she considered his request. If the daily flowers were any indication of his tenacity, she didn't see any other option. "Okay, I have an hour for lunch. But don't you have a job to get back to?"

He shrugged. "Taking a little longer for one lunch won't matter."

Robert buzzed. "Send him in."

Monty picked up his briefcase and entered Robert's office.

Cindy busied herself with the stack of work in front of her and was ready to punch in the final total on the current spread-sheet when Glen Evans arrived.

"Hi," he purred, standing much too close to the front of her desk for her liking.

She buzzed Robert. "Glen Evans is here for his appointment."

Instead of taking a seat, he continued to stand in front of her desk while she attempted to work. She tried to ignore him, but he planted his hip against the side of the desk, half sitting on the corner. She heard the shuffle of his shoes as he crossed his ankles.

"So, since I should be finished with Rob around lunchtime, how about joining me?"

"Sorry, I'm afraid I'm busy for lunch." She smiled politely, then noticed Monty standing behind Glen, who was still lean-ing on her desk.

Monty cleared his throat, startling Glen and causing him to stand. The two of them stood facing each other, sizing each other up like a pair of bantam roosters. Cindy bit her bottom lip.

Fortunately, Robert chose that moment to buzz and tell Cindy that he was ready to see Glen.

Monty's eyes followed Glen until the door closed, making Cindy wonder what was going through his head. He faced her again. "It's only eleven-thirty. I'll be back at noon, if that's okay with you."

"Yes, that will be fine."

He nodded, and she watched him until he disappeared into the elevator, praying she'd done the right thing.

❧

Monty stood outside the building and inhaled a deep, deep breath of fresh air. He could expand his lungs all he wanted, and it didn't hurt anymore. He smiled with the pure joy of freedom to breathe.

With a quick glance at the time, he pulled his cellular phone out of his pocket. He opened the car door and, sitting with his legs sticking out, rescheduled his lunchtime appointment, called his office for his messages, and caught up on a few calls. At noon, rather than going up and making a pest of himself, in case she wasn't ready, he phoned from the parking lot.

"Good morning. Mr. Blackmore's office," Cindy answered in the sweet, melodic voice that had filled his dreams since the accident.

"Hi, it's Monty. It's afternoon now. Available for lunch yet?"

"I'm not sure. One moment please." Music came on the line as she put him on hold. He smiled, admiring her professional phone manners.

"Yes, I can go now, and Robert told me to take an extra half hour. Did you have something to do with that?"

With the phone against his ear, Monty headed back into the building the moment she said she could go.

"Me? Never. I'll be right there," he said, already halfway up the elevator.

"Great. I'll need just a couple of minutes to finish what I'm doing and . . ." She paused for a second. "Can you hold again? I have another call coming in." The elevator continued to rise, and the door opened at the same time as Cindy came back on the line. "Sorry about that. I'll be ready by the time you get here. Okay?"

"Fine by me."

He stood in front of her, but she hadn't noticed him yet.

"Bye," she said into the phone in her hand as she raised her head. She jumped when she saw him.

"Bye," he said into the cellular phone. He snapped it shut and tucked it into his breast pocket.

Cindy glared at the phone in her hand and hastily hung it up. "Very funny," she grumbled.

Monty grinned. "You said you'd be ready when I arrived."

"Just for that, I should take that extra half an hour to comb my hair." She reached under her desk to pick up her purse and rose to leave. Monty noticed the other secretaries watching them, smiling. He nodded and winked, causing one of them to blush, then he followed behind Cindy to the elevator.

&

After she stepped inside the open elevator door, Cindy turned to face Monty, finding herself exactly eye to eye with him. Considering her heels, that made Monty about five-foot-ten. Not that he was short, but after spending so much time with Troy, she wasn't used to it anymore.

He blinked but said nothing.

Monty held the door open as she got into his car. The new blue Mercedes was spotless, inside and out. She ran her hand over the soft leather upholstery. "Nice," she mumbled, checking out the rest of the interior. She'd never been inside a car like this before. "I guess the yellow one must have been written off by the insurance company."

He smiled at her description of his state-of-the-art car. "Yes, it was. I decided to get something with an automatic transmission."

"I couldn't help but notice you have a bit of a limp. Will it go away?"

His cute little grin disappeared. "No. In addition to a number of pins to hold me together, one leg is now a little shorter than the other one. But I can walk, which is more than they first expected. Do you have a favorite restaurant in the area, or should I choose?"

"Anything you choose is fine." Cindy forced herself to smile. She didn't go out often, especially just for lunch, because this was one way of saving money for her college courses in the fall.

He steered into the parking lot of a restaurant where the price of one lunch would pay for nearly a semester's worth of textbooks.

On the way in, she couldn't help but notice his pronounced

limp, nor could she stop herself from looking down when he spoke to the hostess. The sole of one of his shoes looked thicker than the other.

Once they were seated and their orders taken, Monty leaned forward in his chair, rested his elbows on the table, and cradled his coffee cup in his palms. "This probably sounds like a line, but I want to know everything there is to know about you."

She could understand his curiosity, given the circumstances. "I don't know what to say. I don't really do anything interesting."

Monty smiled, returned the cup to its saucer, and leaned back in his chair. "I doubt that. Not everyone would do what you did."

She knew he was referring to that night five months ago. "I have my Industrial First Aid ticket, so it was a natural thing to do. In fact, I had my first aid bag right beside me at the time. I was just on my way home from a practice. We didn't win the trophy, but we did place second."

He raised his eyebrows but said nothing, so Cindy continued.

"Many companies need employees with industrial first aid certification rather than just simple St. John's Ambulance training. I don't know how it started, but once a year there's a big competition between company teams. We set up phony emergencies to practice, and I'm on a team with some of the guys from the last place I worked before Circuits, Inc. It's nice to keep in touch."

He smiled. "Yes, it would be."

Again, he didn't comment further, so Cindy prattled on about her first aid team and the funny things that sometimes happened at the practices. His attention never once wavered until their lunches arrived.

Unsure of what to do in front of a stranger, Cindy steeled her nerve and bowed her head despite being in a public restaurant, meaning to pause for a quick moment of silent prayer before eating.

"Cindy?"

She blushed and opened her eyes. "Sorry, I didn't mean to embarrass you."

When he reached across the table to rest his hand on hers, she tried not to flinch. "Can we give thanks together? I do have a lot to be thankful for."

Unable to speak, she nodded. He bowed his head and closed his eyes, so she did the same. He gave her fingers a gentle squeeze before speaking barely loud enough for her to hear in the public setting.

"Dear Lord, thank You for this day, for the blessings You've bestowed upon us, and for the life You've given us. We thank You for this food we're about to eat and pray for Your continuing guidance and blessings in the days to come. Amen." He squeezed her fingers again, then released her hand.

She nodded and mumbled an "amen," then fumbled with her fork. Of all her preconceived ideas about Monty, that he would be a Christian was not one of them.

"Now where were we? I believe you were telling me about coming in second place in that competition."

"Uh, yes," she mumbled.

"I know it's a difficult and grueling course. You must be proud of yourself."

"Not really. The skills are good to know."

Silence hung in the air.

"So, what else do you do with yourself? I already asked Robert if you were married. I hope you don't mind."

She shook her head.

"I'd like to get to know you better. Unless you're already seeing someone."

Again, she shook her head. The only male she'd spent time with lately was Troy and she simply didn't have those kinds of feelings for him. Besides, lately Troy had been seeing a lot of Erin, which, in a way, she found a relief.

Conversation drifted to general topics, allowing her to relax, but inside, her mind was doing cartwheels. Rather than talk about herself, she had so much she wanted to ask him.

When the conversation lagged, he again steered it toward more personal questions. "So, what do you do for fun? What do you do with yourself in the evenings? What are your hobbies and interests?"

"Besides the first aid thing, I like to go hiking. It's a wonderful way to enjoy the beauty of God's creation. "

He sighed, staring off into space for a few seconds. "I obviously haven't been able to do much of anything since the accident. I think I miss hiking most of all. Where do you like to go? There's a great trail up the mountain at Golden Ears Provincial Park that's a real challenge. I've yet to try the one that goes to the peak. Maybe someday we could go together?"

She tried not to let her mouth drop open. She would have guessed his tastes leaned toward an expensive health club. "You like to hike?"

He nodded. "I find the trails a great place to escape to get my head together."

Cindy enjoyed a brisk walk in the forest. Hiking was also cheap, the only cost being the boots and backpack, which lasted for years, plus the gas to get out of town.

"Want to go hiking together? Although, I'll be going pretty slow, compared to what you're no doubt used to. And I'll have to stick to the level ground. I've been cooped up so long, I think I'll go stark raving mad if I don't get out soon. Most of all, I'd really enjoy your company."

"I guess we could go slow and easy, maybe take a lunch and make a day of it."

The words barely out of her mouth, Cindy realized what she had just committed herself to. Instead of convincing him to stop sending more flowers, she had obligated herself into spending an entire day with him.

She folded her hands in front of her on the tabletop. "I've answered all your questions. Turnabout is fair play. Besides hiking, what do you do for fun? So far, we've only talked about me."

Monty laid his fork down to thoughtfully swirl the last of his coffee at the bottom of the cup.

"Lately I've spent most of my time working. Aside from hiking, I sometimes go sailing when I can get away for a day on the weekend, which isn't often anymore." He paused to drink the last sip of his coffee. "I was doing some work on the boat the day of the accident." He laughed without mirth for a second. "I fell in, and, boy, was that water cold. I had to either drive home soaking wet and freezing or strip down to my underwear with the heat up full blast. Good thing I found an old pair of shorts on the boat." He smiled, and his ears reddened. "Afterwards I was pretty embarrassed, but at the time, though, I didn't care. I really thought I was going to die."

His laughter disappeared. "I really thought that was the end, Cindy. I don't think there's any way to say thank you for something like that, but if it wasn't for you and God's timing, I wouldn't be on this earth today."

Cindy gulped. Monty reached across the table, touched her hand, and gave it a little squeeze. His tender gesture reminded her so much of the pitiful way he had tried to do the same thing in the car that night. The memory almost brought tears to her eyes. "I don't know what to say," she choked out.

"I'm sorry, I really meant to keep today lighthearted. I think I'd better get you back to work."

They made pleasant small talk until they reached her office. He parked the car and escorted her to the main entrance. Before she had a chance to say good-bye, he clasped one hand between his larger ones. "May I call you at home?"

She pulled her hand away, nodded, and hurried inside.

Alone in the elevator, she leaned against the wall, trying to will her heart from pounding so hard. She had expected a stilted and awkward conversation, but instead, she had enjoyed herself. Making arrangements to see him again had fallen into place naturally. However, seeing him again was a very bad idea.

Before she completed her industrial first aid course, the instructor had recommended a book to the class. She had been so impressed with it that she'd decided to buy it rather than check it out from the library. One of the chapters described common responses of a victim toward their rescuer.

From his reaction to their first meeting in the office and his wanting to somehow pay her back, to the flowers, to their get-to-know-you lunch, he displayed the classic symptoms in the correct order, according to the book. The book cautioned rescuers that in a male/female situation, it was common for many victims to mistake their extreme gratitude for affection, erroneously believing themselves to be in love with the rescuer. The projected outcome of such a relationship was doomed from the start, having been based on unrealistic or false expectations.

The elevator door swooshed open. Brenda, Melinda, Ann, and Susan stopped what they were doing, lifted their arms at the same time to study their watches, and shook their heads in unison. Cindy wondered how much they'd practiced their little performance while she was gone.

"Very funny," she groused as she marched to her desk.

Cindy squeezed her eyes shut at the onslaught of four voices bombarding her at once.

"What's he like?"

"Did he take you somewhere really nice?"

"He sure is good looking, isn't he?"

"What did he say?"

"Is he as nice as he looks?"

"Did he ask you out again?"

Cindy threw her hands up. "Stop it, all of you!" Four pairs of eyes burned into her. "We had a nice lunch, and yes, I'm going to see him again. Okay?" She tried her best to ignore them and resumed her work. Before long, they took the hint. As she typed, her mind ran through a mental checklist of her meager selection of shoes, and which ones had the lowest heels, then she kicked herself for thinking about such a thing.

❧

"Are you running away from home or something?"

Cindy sat in the middle of her bedroom floor surrounded by all the hiking supplies she had just pulled out of her bedroom closet. Partly because of her new job and partly because of spending so much time with Troy, she hadn't been hiking since last year. She hadn't realized until she talked to Monty how much she missed it.

"I'm going hiking next weekend with Monty."

Erin snorted. "Sounds like fun," she said, not at all sounding like she meant it. While Cindy shared many interests and activities with Erin, hiking was not one of them.

Cindy pushed everything to the side. "I guess it's time for me to make dinner."

She had everything nearly ready and was about to dump the water out of the cooked noodles when the phone rang.

"Hi, Cindy, it's Monty. What are you doing?"

She nearly dumped the noodles on the floor. "I'm making supper. How about you?"

"I'm just finishing up at the office, and I was thinking of asking you to join me for dinner."

"You're too late. I've already started cooking dinner for myself and my roommate."

"Oh. Is there any way I could convince you to join me?"

Cindy didn't need this. As much as she enjoyed his company, she couldn't see him again other than the hike that she'd already committed herself to. "Sorry, Monty, not this time."

"When then? I'm free anytime you are. Tomorrow?"

"No, not tomorrow."

"Friday?"

Cindy squeezed her eyes shut. She definitely didn't need this. Obviously she had led him to the wrong conclusion and now she needed to make her intentions clear. "Tell you what. I'm making lasagna, why don't you come here? We can talk."

"Sounds great!" His enthusiasm almost made her choke. "I can be out of here in five minutes."

After giving him directions, she hung up the phone and continued assembling the lasagna. When she slid the pan into the oven, she went to tell Erin what she'd done.

Erin was hanging up the phone. "I knew you were making a big lasagna, so I invited Troy."

Cindy slapped her hand to her forehead and groaned. "Monty phoned, and I have something to discuss with him, so I invited him, too. Now what?"

Erin rested her hands on her hips. "Won't there be enough to feed four?"

Erin obviously had no concept of the amount of lasagna Troy could eat, a fact Cindy had learned the hard way. "I was going to make a salad, so I guess I'll just make a bigger salad and some quick instant pudding for dessert. Do we have any of that spray whipped cream left?"

Erin grinned and shook her head, which meant that Erin had used the rest of the can to make fancy coffees when Troy came over last night.

Cindy hurried to add more volume to their meal and was nearly finished when a knock on the door stopped her.

It was Monty, holding a paper bag with the logo of a nearby bakery. Unlike earlier in the day, he stood a couple of inches taller than she did.

"I brought something extra for dinner," he said as he looked down at her feet, which were cuddled up in her flat-soled bunny slippers. A frivolous item she never would have chosen by herself, they were a gift from Erin, a joke meant to take her down a peg or two after she accepted the lofty position of executive secretary. She wore them constantly because her feet were always cold in the drafty old house.

Monty grinned. "Nice slippers."

Blushing, she took the bag from him. "I'd like to introduce you to my roommate and best friend, Erin."

He extended his hand. "Pleased to meet you, Erin," he said cordially, nodding as their hands touched.

No sooner had they closed the door, when another knock sounded. As soon as Erin opened the door, Troy sauntered past them and flopped down on the couch. "What a day!"

When he spotted Monty, his eyes widened, and he stood. "Excuse me, I didn't see you."

Monty walked to Troy and shook his hand while Cindy introduced them. The difference between the two of them was like night and day.

In addition to Troy's fair complexion, long wavy blond hair, and the bluest eyes Cindy had ever seen, his boyish grin nearly sent women into a swoon. As usual, Troy wore snug jeans and a baggy sweatshirt, and his damp hair showed that he had been home and showered before his arrival.

In contrast to Troy's height, Monty was barely average. His dark complexion matched his nearly black hair, which was meticulously cut and perfectly combed back. When he smiled, he radiated elegance and dignity. Monty still wore his tailored suit and tie, showing that he had just come from work.

The timer on the stove dinged, so Cindy excused herself. Monty followed.

Cindy reached into the cupboard for the plates. "I'm sorry, Monty. It appears that neither one of us knew the other had invited a guest."

"Not a problem. Can I set the table for you?"

She pointed in the direction of the cutlery drawer. "Do you work late often?"

"Yes. I like to work in peace and quiet after everyone is gone, and it's not unusual for me to be there till midnight or later to finish up."

"Your card said you're the systems manager. I don't even know what it is you do."

"I write and manage various business programs, but I started out doing computer games. I still do some, but not as many as I used to."

"Computer games? You make money doing that?"

He nodded. "I'm working on one right now about teenagers cleaning their rooms. The dust bunnies under the bed come equipped with laser cannons. The pile of clothes and dirty socks and other teen paraphernalia builds until it either destroys the room or it gets cleaned up. Which seldom happens, by the way, just like real life."

He gave her a mischievous grin. "I always give the staff a couple of hours to test the games for suggestions or improvements. The business programs are boring. They don't offer to test those. That would mean work."

She couldn't imagine the soft-spoken man in the pristine suit beside her making battle games about killer dust bunnies.

Cindy pulled the lasagna out of the oven. "Can you call Erin and Troy?"

Monty disappeared for a few seconds and came back alone, his cheeks slightly darkened. "They look like they're busy, and I didn't want to disturb them."

He remained in the kitchen while she scuffed into the living room, where Troy sat on the couch with Erin in his lap, locked together in a fervent kiss, heedless of the world around them. She squeezed her eyes shut tightly, imagining what Monty must have thought.

She marched back into the kitchen. "Cover your ears," she grumbled. She sucked in a deep breath and yelled, "Suppertime!" at the top of her lungs.

Monty and Cindy could hear the shuffling from the kitchen.

"Nice touch," Monty whispered.

Red-faced, Erin and Troy entered the kitchen and quietly sat at the table. Already knowing the routine, Troy bowed his head while Erin led a prayer thanking God for their meal.

Erin immediately started the conversation by griping about the traffic on the way home.

five

Monty listened politely to Erin but watched Cindy. In the informal atmosphere of her own home, she was even more delightful than she had been at lunchtime. Her smoky gray eyes sparkled with laughter while she teased Erin as Erin continued to complain without missing a beat.

At first, Erin's boyfriend freely joined in with the banter, but when Erin commented on Monty's car, Monty noted a change in him. He was silent so long, that both women froze and stared when Troy finally spoke again.

"So that's your Mercedes parked out front. I was wondering what a car like that was doing in this neighborhood."

Monty faced Troy. He'd noticed the status of the neighborhood when he pulled up. The houses were getting old, but most of the homes were in fairly decent condition, although a few yards looked a bit shabby and some of the homes could have used a fair amount of repair, not to mention a few coats of paint. While not completely run down, this was definitely a neighborhood for the less affluent. He suspected most of the occupants of the houses were elderly and had lived here most of their lives or were young couples with children, unable to afford anything better.

"Looks new." Troy glanced out the window, his eyes narrowed.

Seeing Cindy's humble home and meager furnishings, he didn't want to make an issue of his expensive car. "Yes, I've only had it a couple of months."

Troy didn't comment further, but Monty felt Troy's eyes almost burning into him. Monty didn't want to feel self-conscious or have to worry about Erin's boyfriend. He was there to get to know Cindy better.

He turned to Cindy. "This lasagna is a real treat. It's not very interesting cooking for one and by the time I get home, it's the last thing I feel like doing. This is delicious. Thank you, Cindy."

"Why do you put in such long hours?" she asked.

He shuffled in the chair, deliberately disregarding Troy. "I don't know. I guess I have nothing better to do." As he concentrated on Cindy's face, he wondered if that was about to change.

Troy lounged back in the chair, but his stony expression denied any impression of leisure. "What do you do for a living, Monty, that it keeps you working late so often?"

Monty turned in the chair. While they were ordinary questions, something in Troy's voice made him feel like he was being interviewed, although he didn't know for what. "My job is kind of hard to describe. At the moment I'm preparing a project for Robert, Cindy's boss."

Troy's lips tightened. "Is that how you met Cindy?"

Monty saw Cindy squirm in her chair. He didn't want to discuss that night not so long ago, and Cindy didn't look like she did, either. Besides, the first time he saw Cindy wasn't exactly what he would term "meeting" her. "Yes, we met through Robert."

"How do you know Robert?"

The questioning had just crossed over the line from interviewing to interrogation, and Monty didn't like it. However, he didn't want to show his irritation in front of Cindy. He wasn't sure how to answer Troy's question, nor did he figure he should have to.

"Just through business. Why do you ask?"

Troy's brows knotted and he crossed his arms. "What kind of deal do you have cooking with Blackmore?"

Monty crossed his arms as well and leaned back in his chair. He didn't want to try to figure out what was going on or why Erin's boyfriend was acting like a jerk. He wanted to put an end to Troy's cross-examination and spend his time with Cindy.

He put on his best business smile. "Hopefully I'll be re-designing the computer networking system and reconfiguring the database." Monty started contemplating reconfiguring Troy's database.

Troy eyed him up and down, his gaze lingering on Monty's favorite tie. "In other words, you're a computer geek." He glanced out the window toward Monty's car. "It figures."

Before Monty could respond, Cindy stood. "I think it's time to clear the table."

Monty stood as well. "I'll help you do the dishes."

At the mention of work, Troy and Erin disappeared into the living room and the television came on.

Cindy and Monty chatted amicably for a short time, but after a short silence, Cindy spoke again. Her voice lowered, and she wouldn't look at him. "I'm so sorry about Troy. He's not normally like that."

"It's not your fault. It's okay."

"It's not okay. I don't know what's gotten into him."

"I was wondering if he was your brother or something."

"I don't have a brother."

"Do you have a sister then? Tell me about your family."

Cindy stared out the window above the kitchen sink. "I was an only child. My parents were killed in a car accident when I was young, so my grandmother raised me, and then she died when I was seventeen. I have no other relatives except for an aunt and uncle in Arizona. I send them a letter at Christmas."

"I'm sorry. If you were only seventeen, who did you stay with when your grandmother died?"

"No one." She scrubbed a dish far more than necessary and wouldn't look at him. "I only had a few months until I reached legal age, so instead of going into a group home, some people from my church vouched for me and offered sponsorship. As soon as I reached legal age, I managed on my own."

His gut clenched. He knew what it was like to be young and alone, only he hadn't had anyone to help him.

"This duplex belonged to my grandmother. There wasn't

much money, so when I graduated from high school, I took the first job I could get. I've had a few tough breaks, but through God's grace, everything is really coming together. I'm still not sure how I got this job, but I'm managing to save enough money to take a few night school courses in the fall so I can learn all I already should know."

She turned to him with such a big smile that the words he was about to speak caught in his throat.

"I still don't know what a systems manager does, but you're obviously into computer programming. I guess you had to go to school for that, too."

Monty smiled. "Actually, yes, I've taken a few courses, but I made the title up. I started the company when I was twenty-two, and I had to think of something to encompass all that I did when I was a one-man show. Even though I've expanded, the title still fits."

Her smile dropped. "You own the company? How old are you?"

"I'm twenty-nine."

She plunged her hands back into the soapy water. "For only twenty-nine, you're doing very well for yourself."

"Things haven't always been this way. I come from what people in this end of town still call the wrong side of the tracks. I've worked very hard to get where I am."

"You'd get further if you didn't spend so much on all those flowers."

"Not really." He grinned.

Cindy didn't return his smile. "I'm being serious, you know."

He didn't want to talk about stopping the flowers. Now he wanted to keep sending them more than ever. He couldn't do much for her, but continuing to send her flowers showed her how special she was and that seemed like a good start.

Monty reached to put a plate away in the cupboard. "We need to talk about our hike. I'm tied up this Saturday, and of course Sunday is church, but I'm free next Saturday. If we leave early, we can take our time, have lunch on the trail, then when we're done, we can treat ourselves to a greasy burger and fries for dinner."

Finally, he managed to get a smile out of her. "I don't know why that sounds good, but it does. Who's driving? You may not want to take your nice new car on the gravel road."

"If you're offering, sure, you can drive. Got a pen and paper? I'll give you my address."

With her hands still immersed in the soapy water, Cindy nodded to her junk drawer. "My address book is in there, right on top. Just write it in."

Monty pulled the drawer open, laid her address book on the counter, pulled his glasses out of his pocket, and paged to the "S" section. "I see you already have my office number in here. I'm flattered." He neatly wrote in his address and home phone number.

Cindy studied the suds. "I took it off your business card," she mumbled.

When he finished writing his address in her book, Monty stood and returned his glasses to his pocket. "I'm afraid I've got to be heading home. I still have a lot of work to do before my meeting tomorrow morning, and I'm also working on an accounting program for a new client. I have to get it done while it's fresh in my mind."

They walked out of the kitchen, through the living room, where Erin and Troy were on the couch, still smooching.

Cindy retrieved Monty's suit jacket from the closet. "Now if I could only get Troy to leave," she whispered.

"Does this happen often?"

"No. Even though Erin has known Troy almost as long as I have, they only recently started dating."

Monty wondered if an earthquake would separate Erin and Troy, but he was grateful they were so engaged. This way he could say good night to Cindy at the door without interruption or distraction, or worse, knowing he was being watched.

Before he left, Monty grasped her hands in his, then backed

up a bit and craned his neck slightly backward, annoyed as never before by his lousy vision. "Good night, Cindy. Thank you for dinner, especially on short notice."

She smiled back. "You're welcome."

Monty would have liked to kiss her good night, but they didn't know each other well enough for that. Hopefully, however, that would soon change. He nodded and left, closing the door gently behind him, and walked out to his car, doing his best to minimize his constant limp.

As he started the car, he wondered what kind of flowers he could send her tomorrow.

❧

Cindy couldn't help herself as she peeked through the blinds, watching Monty's stilted walk to the car. Despite the knowledge that anything he felt for her was a misplaced sense of obligation, she couldn't help but like him. She wondered if they had met any other way if things could have worked out between them.

Part of her looked forward to their plans for some quiet time in the forest, away from the hustle and bustle of crowds and business. Another part of her mentally kicked herself for getting so distracted that she hadn't told him that seeing him again wasn't a good idea. She didn't want to think of what would happen when reality crashed in on him and he saw her for the person she really was. Plain, ordinary Cindy, the ex-forklift driver.

She didn't want to compare their lifestyles. She didn't care what area of town he came from. The here-and-now was what mattered most, and now he owned a successful business, wore expensive clothes, and drove an expensive car. She didn't want to guess at what kind of home he lived in. Most of all, he no doubt hung around with people who enjoyed the same social status, and that didn't include her.

She owned half a run-down duplex—only because she had inherited it. And the old place was mortgaged to the max because of all the financial trouble she'd been in for so long.

What little furniture she had was old, and she drove a car that was in such poor condition that her mechanic planned his next vacation every time he saw her coming.

Cindy continued to watch through the blinds until his tail lights disappeared around the corner. She was too mad to look at Troy, so she walked straight into her bedroom and shut the door.

Since she couldn't sleep, she pulled out her latest **Heart-song Presents** book and stretched out across the bed to lose her troubles in a story she knew would have a happy ending. She was just getting to the good part when a tap sounded on the door.

Erin stepped in, raised her arms in the air, twirled on her toes, hugged herself, then flopped backward to lean against the wall. "Oh, Cindy!" she sighed. "I'm in love!"

Cindy rolled her eyes. "I don't believe this."

"It's true. I can barely believe it myself." Erin sighed again.

Cindy smacked her open palm on top of the page. "In love or not, I couldn't believe the two of you on the couch. I've never been so embarrassed."

"I'm sorry." Erin stared at her feet and rubbed one toe into the carpet. "Really."

Cindy sighed. "If we must discuss this, do you have any idea how Troy feels about you?"

"He feels the same way. What about you and Monty?" Erin tipped her head to the side. "He's cute. Seems your type, too."

"My type?" Cindy crossed her arms. "And what type would that be?"

"You know. So serious about things. Just like you."

"He's not my type, and you know it."

Erin snorted. "Really? Look at what you're going to do. You and your new beau have plans to trudge through the damp and dirty bushes battling the bugs to go have lunch in the middle of nowhere." Erin raised her hands up in the air, then dropped them to her sides with a slap. "I couldn't think of a better place to go on a date."

"He's not my beau and it's not a date."

Erin snorted again.

"We both thought it was a great idea."

"See?"

Cindy snapped her book shut. "Go to bed, Erin."

&

Another vase of flowers awaited Cindy as she arrived at work. This time the arrangement consisted of a sprig of yellow buttercups, a row of red snapdragons, and a white gardenia. Cindy was beginning to see a pattern. She was also beginning to see that Montgomery Smythe didn't listen well to instruction.

As the week progressed, since she hadn't seen or heard from him except for the daily arrival of the flowers, she no longer felt the urgency of telling him she wouldn't see him again after their hike. However, she couldn't stop thinking about him.

Each day a different variety of flowers arrived, but every day the flowers were the same colors. Red, white, and yellow. If he had a point to make and was trying to pique her curiosity, by Friday, he'd succeeded.

Robert buzzed just after her afternoon coffee break and handed her a large manila envelope marked *Smythe Computer Systems*. "Our lawyer has drawn up this contract for their proposal and I need you to deliver it to Smythe. Go now, and have a nice weekend."

Cindy nodded. Since she hadn't spoken to Monty all week, her worries appeared to have been in vain. Strangely, although she knew it was best, the thought caused her some regret.

As she packed up her desk for the weekend, including today's flowers of one red tulip, one white zinnia, and something that looked like an oversized fluffy dandelion, she felt the eyes of the four secretaries on her back.

"It looks like 'courier' has just been added to my job description. Bye, all." She'd heard enough razzing about the flowers every day, so she deliberately didn't tell them where she was going. As it was, the receptionist downstairs was on a first-name basis with the florist's delivery man.

The address brought Cindy to a downtown high-rise office tower, which held a number of businesses. Inside the door boldly marked "Smythe Computer Systems, Inc.," she found two younger men and a gray-haired lady busily working. Computers, printers, and other high-tech equipment that she didn't recognize lined the walls. Across the room, Monty sat behind a desk in a small private office with windowed walls.

His suit jacket hung across the back of his chair. His tie was pulled open to a wide circle draped around his neck, and the top few buttons on his shirt were undone. His loose cuffs rolled up halfway to his elbows showed the dusting of dark hair on his arms.

A coffee cup sat on the corner of the desk, along with a half-eaten sandwich. Wearing his glasses, he studiously concentrated on his computer screen as he typed. Watching him type so fast, Cindy suspected that Monty typed better than she did.

The woman folded her hands on her desk. "Can I help you?"

"I have an envelope for Mr. Smythe."

The lady smiled curiously and eyed Cindy up and down, leaving Cindy to wonder if maybe Monty didn't get many visitors. The woman dialed Monty's office and spoke to him. He removed his glasses and turned toward her as he hung up the phone. Walking out of his office, he smiled warmly and pulled the knot on his tie tighter.

"This is a pleasant surprise. What brings you around this side of town?"

She handed him the envelope and followed him back into his office, where, once inside, he closed the door. He held the contract at arm's length and craned his neck backward at the same time as he patted his shirt pocket with his other hand. Looking around, he then picked up his glasses off the desk. Once they were perched on his nose, he relaxed and held the paper at a more comfortable distance. "This is good. Except for a few concessions, it's exactly what I wanted." He signed the document and handed it back to Cindy along with a pen.

"What do you want me to do with this?" she asked.

"Witness it." He pointed out a few spots on the contract. "Sign here and here and initial here. All you're doing is swearing that you saw me sign it. And put the date here."

She grinned. "But as a Christian, I don't swear." He returned her grin but didn't comment. As she leaned over the desk to sign, he was so close that she could detect the faint scent of his musky aftershave, even so late in the day. She hastily scribbled her signature and backed up. Monty removed his glasses and laid them back down on the desk.

He seemed unaffected, making her feel foolish. She fumbled with her purse for lack of something to do with her hands. "I think I'd better phone Robert, just in case he wants this back today."

"Be my guest." Monty pushed the phone across the desk and left the office to allow her to make her call in private.

The quick phone call gave her time to calm her rattled nerves. When she opened the door after hanging up, Monty was speaking to one of the other office workers. As soon as he noticed her, he straightened and approached her. His shirt was now buttoned up, the cuffs rolled down and fastened neatly at his wrists, and his tie was pulled all the way to the top and neatly straightened. Unless she imagined it, his hair was also freshly combed.

"He asked me to take it home and bring it in Monday morning."

"Great. If you're not expected back, why don't we go out to dinner while you're here?"

She wanted the opportunity to talk to him in private, but going out for dinner was too intimate a setting to suit Cindy. Besides, she didn't think it would be very nice to allow him to take her out for dinner only to tell him she didn't want to see him again. "I don't know. . . ." Cindy looked at the door, then at her watch. "I have to go to the bank."

"I'm famished, but I hate to dine alone. I wish you'd join me." He smiled, setting off the adorable crinkles at the corners of his eyes, weakening Cindy's resolve.

"I guess," she mumbled.

"It will take me about fifteen minutes to finish up what I'm doing, if you don't mind waiting. Then I'll show you to the nearest bank, and we can have an early dinner." Monty nodded toward the chair beside her. "You can stay right here in my office while I finish this."

She didn't like his expectant expression. The man wore his heart on his sleeve. She strengthened her resolve to tell him tonight, before he got any more wrong ideas. Cindy hesitated, but she didn't know what else to do. "Okay."

With that, he put his glasses back on and continued typing. Within the predicted fifteen minutes, he stood, slipped on his suit jacket, and tidied up his desk. "Done. Let's go."

The receptionist spoke as he opened the door. "When will you be back?"

"Monday."

All three staff members stopped working to look at their wristwatches.

"Is everything all right, Montgomery?" the receptionist asked.

"Just fine," he answered. "Good night, all." With that, Monty rested his hand lightly on the small of Cindy's back and ushered her out the door.

six

"I gather you don't usually leave early?"

Monty nodded. "Agnes enjoys taking great pains to catch me working late and then giving me a rough time about it. Lately, I've been leaving around seven o'clock, but since everything at the office is connected to my home by modem, I finish up there." He shrugged his shoulders. "Don't ask me why I let her do this to me. After all, I'm the boss."

He stopped talking as a man walked past them in the hallway and nodded in greeting. "When Monday morning comes, I won't hear the end of this from her." He pushed the button for the elevator. "The bank is in a mall just around the corner. We could walk in less time than we could drive."

Inside the elevator, they again stood exactly eye to eye. Cindy suddenly faced forward. If she had known this was going to happen, she would have chosen flatter shoes. "I think I should put the contract in my car. I don't want to take a chance losing or bending it."

When she opened the car door, the scent of flowers wafted out. "By the way, you said you weren't going to send me any more flowers."

"Did I say that? I don't remember promising."

"Very funny," she mumbled.

He had the nerve to grin.

"What do I have to say or do to get you to stop sending all these flowers?"

"Don't you like flowers?"

"Of course I like flowers."

"So what's the problem? I enjoy sending you a few flowers from time to time."

Every day did not constitute "a few," but recognizing the

69

signs of a losing battle, Cindy gave up. "A little bird told me that you didn't finish your lunch, so I guess we should go get something to eat right after I deposit my paycheck."

His cheeks darkened slightly. "I guess I got so lost in what I was doing, I didn't notice the time. And for the record, my office isn't usually such a mess, but I'm pushing a deadline. I'm not going to lie. I'm famished. Do you have a favorite restaurant I can take you to?"

A hamburger in the small food court inside the mall would have suited her purposes just fine. "Anything is okay with me."

"There's a nice little Japanese place nearby, the kind where you go into a little room and take off your shoes. How's that sound?"

It sounded far too intimate. "Well, I don't know. . . ."

"It's not far, just down that end of the mall and around the corner."

She opened her mouth to protest, but changed her mind. Someplace within walking distance was probably better. That way, she wouldn't face an awkward situation with transportation or have to spend more time with him once she said what she had to say. "Okay, which way?"

"To the right."

As they walked through the mall toward the bank, Cindy couldn't help but be aware of the uneven pace that accompanied his constant limp. She took extra care to walk slowly, hoping it wasn't too obvious that she was slowing down for him.

He sat at a bench while she ran into the bank, then they continued on their way to a small Japanese restaurant that had entrances both from the mall and the outside.

The hostess, attired in a floral-patterned Japanese geisha costume, escorted them to a quaint little room with rice paper walls, hand-painted with scenes of flowers and dragons and people in old-world costumes. Twangy oriental music played softly in the background. The hostess indicated where to leave their shoes, and they slid into place at the low table.

Cindy noticed that Monty slid in very slowly, then exhaled

in relief as he straightened his left leg. She'd done her best to ignore his constant limp, which was a poignant reminder that his accident really hadn't been all that long ago.

After presenting the menus, their waitress left them alone in the small cubicle.

Instead of reading the menu, Cindy studied the room. Even though the walls between the tables were made of thin paper, they still provided an atmosphere of privacy. She heard the low murmur of voices, but couldn't make out individual conversations.

She'd hardly been out to dinner at all in the past year, and lately the only person she'd been out with besides Erin was Troy. In the private atmosphere, if she had been with Troy, by now he would be trying to play footsie under the table since they had to take off their shoes.

Across the table from her, with his glasses perched efficiently on his nose, Monty studied the menu. "Feel exotic?" he asked without lifting his head. "Ever tried sushi?"

Cindy abandoned her analysis of the room and picked up her menu. Except for sushi, which she knew was raw fish, she had no idea what any of the menu items were. "I think you'd better order for me. I've never been to a place like this before."

He lowered his chin and peered at her over the tops of his glasses. "Really? My, but you're trusting. Well, you asked for it." At his impish grin, Cindy's heart beat a little faster.

When the waitress returned, he gave her their orders and returned his glasses to his pocket. A few minutes later, the waitress brought them a painted ceramic teapot and two small ceramic cups without handles.

Cindy sniffed at the fragrant steam. "What is this?"

"A special blend of green tea, mostly jasmine, I believe. You have to let the tea steep for a few more minutes. Watch out, it's very hot. When it's ready, be careful to pour slowly so you don't get tea leaves in your cup."

After waiting a sufficient amount of time, she cautiously tasted the tea and discovered she liked it. To her surprise, she enjoyed the entire meal, which came in small unidentifiable servings, one item at a time. This made the entire dinner stretch out to an unbelievable amount of time. Monty made a lame joke about the necessity of saying grace over each new arrival, even though they didn't. Each course amounted to little more than a few bites.

In the neutral atmosphere, Cindy allowed herself to relax. Despite the fact that Monty seemed to be very serious-minded, she enjoyed his company. Unlike her time with Troy, she didn't have to constantly be on her guard to fend off any advances, however playful. Even though Troy's teasing always started out as fun, he didn't know when to quit, and after awhile she got more than a little tired it. Not having to worry about any hidden agenda, Cindy could simply relax and be herself with Monty. After all, she had nothing to lose. By the time the evening ended, if he was even still interested, she would tell him how she felt, and they would part friends. She chatted amicably, enjoying herself more than she had in a long time.

&

Monty sat back, listening to Cindy talk, entranced. He'd never met anyone like her before. She was exactly as she claimed to be. She didn't flirt with him, in fact, the opposite. Everything she said and did showed no ulterior motives or designs. She appeared to simply enjoy her evening out. At least he hoped she was enjoying herself as much as he was. Most of all, she didn't look up or down at him.

She didn't treat him like the lowlife illegitimate son of some hooker or drug addict, which all indications had led him to believe himself to be. He had no desire to dig into his records to find out that his suspicions were true. Having run away from the social services system enough times as a youth, often living on the streets until he was too scared or hungry to take any more chances, he'd been bounced around through a high number of foster homes, both good and bad, until he reached legal age. He'd spent the majority of his life on the wrong side of the tracks. She didn't care about his past.

Now that he had become a success, those who previously ignored him or showed their disdain appeared out of the woodwork. For awhile, some of his business contacts and even one woman he thought he recognized as a neighbor had appeared in the strangest places, giving him sideways glances and hints that made it impossible to mistake their motives. He wasn't interested in those types of people.

However, Cindy didn't fall at his feet or try to impress him, flirt with him, or play feminine games. He had been perfectly honest with her, and without giving her a notarized bank statement of his net worth or financial standing, she was intelligent enough to figure out that he was well on the way to being independently wealthy. She not only did not care, she appeared to have created a distance between them at that discovery, and he admired her for her strength of character. He could let his guard down and simply be himself.

Unfortunately, he had the impression that if Robert hadn't given her the contract to deliver, she wouldn't be with him now. Being with Cindy and joining in the lighthearted conversation made him realize he hadn't been able to sit back and really relax in years, or perhaps in his entire life.

He couldn't help but admire her solidness of faith. Several of the foster homes where he'd lived had been Christian homes, and they constantly told him that God loved him, even dragged him to church despite his unwilling attitude. He hadn't believed anything they said. Instead, he'd felt God had abandoned him—until the day of his accident, when he realized God had been with him all along and he had been the one pushing God away, not the other way around.

Despite the situations in which he found himself, in hindsight, he could see God had always been with him, keeping him safe. When he made his decision to apply himself and make something of his life, he thought he'd fallen into every opportunity on his own. Looking back, it was God who had opened every door. Wide. Even when he'd been on death's doorstep, God again reached out to touch him by sending Cindy just for the short time he needed her, before she disappeared.

And now, when he'd given up on finding her, God blessed him again, putting Cindy in his path. This time he wouldn't lose her.

He smiled at yet another of Cindy's amusing anecdotes, wishing the evening could last forever. However, since they'd had dessert and finished a second pot of tea, he had no excuse to keep her any longer. He could hardly wait until the following weekend, the day of their planned hike.

Monty slipped on his shoes, then stepped back to allow Cindy to do the same. The woman, although far from dainty, exhibited a grace beyond physical size. He extended one hand to offer some support, even though he knew if she did more than merely steady herself on him, he'd never be able to maintain his balance and hold her up. Just to have her touch him, he decided to risk possible embarrassment.

Absently, she slid her hand into his, then leaned slightly as she slipped one foot into her shoe, then the other. Thankfully, he managed to maintain his balance.

When she straightened, Monty didn't let go of her hand. At her little tug, he continued to hold on until her eyebrows scrunched and she stared at their joined hands. When she tugged again, he reluctantly released her. For a few unguarded moments, it had felt right, just to touch her, even in such an innocent and harmless way.

Once outside, he walked as slowly as possible without appearing obvious in his desire to simply want to spend more time with her. She slowed her pace to match his without comment or protest. Too soon, they arrived at her car parked alongside the curb in front of his office building.

"Can I drive you home?"

She raised one eyebrow and stared at him strangely. "Drive me home? Is there something wrong with your car? Did you want to borrow mine?"

Monty felt his cheeks heat up. He'd never fished for an

invitation from a woman before, but he hadn't achieved his present success by being insecure. "No, it's fine. It's still in the underground parking at the office. I could always take a cab back later to pick it up. I thought that since the night is still young, we could spend more time talking together."

"Well, there is something I need to discuss with you, now that you mention it."

He could hardly wait to find out what she wanted to say. "Where do you want to go?"

Cindy lowered her head as she dug in her purse for her keys. "After two pots of tea, I don't feel like going out for coffee and donuts. Why don't you come to my house?"

He smiled. He hadn't forgotten where she lived. "Sure. I'll only be a few minutes."

He hurried as best he could to his car, then followed her through the downtown area and the older section of town to her small duplex.

While he parked, he made a mental note that the lights were still out, which indicated that Erin was not yet home. He waited behind Cindy as she unlocked the front door.

She turned her head to glance over her shoulder. "Wait a minute. I'll turn on the light for you." While he waited, Cindy stepped inside to the right, and before his eyes, her arms shot out to the sides, and she started to topple.

Without thinking, he dashed up the two steps and grabbed her around the waist so she wouldn't fall. Pain shot through his left leg and it buckled at the strain of trying to catch and hold her weight. He gritted his teeth against the stab of pain as he started to go down along with Cindy, his arms still locked around her waist. So he wouldn't land on the floor on top of her, he pushed her sideways and leaned deliberately to the right. Together, they thumped into the wall and somehow remained upright.

He couldn't see anything more than her vague outline in the dark and he certainly couldn't make out any of her features without his glasses on, but he could feel every inch of her as he sandwiched her between himself and the wall. The pain in his leg subsided to a tolerable level as soon as he straightened his knee and took the majority of his weight off of it. As soon as he could, he stood, leaving only an inch between them. With his hands resting firmly on the feminine indent of her waist, even though he felt like a caveman pinning her against the wall, he couldn't make himself back up. His heart pounded in his chest as he fought the urge to close that inch. Instead of doing anything ungentlemanly in this intimate position, Monty lifted one hand to graze his fingertips along her cheek.

"You okay?" he asked, his voice coming out much more husky than it should have.

"Erin's shoe. . . ," Cindy mumbled, her voice trailing off and doing strange things to his insides.

Inwardly, Monty kicked himself for not being able to wear contacts, nor was he a candidate for laser surgery. His eyes had become accustomed to the semidark, and even though her features were a blur, in the dim light reflecting through the window, he could see Cindy's slightly parted lips and her wide shimmering eyes staring directly into his. He was lost; he couldn't help himself.

His eyes drifted shut, and he tipped his head to kiss her. The second his lips touched hers, the light flashed on.

"Cindy? The door was wide open and. . ." Erin's voice trailed and died.

Cindy's head turned abruptly at the same time as they both flinched and separated. Monty dropped his hands, stepped back, and turned around.

He blinked against the shock of the sudden light. Erin stood in the doorway, her eyes and mouth open wide, and behind her stood Troy, towering over Erin, glaring at him, his lips pressed tightly together.

seven

Monty backed up to allow Cindy to step away from the wall. She cleared her throat and smoothed her hair. Her voice came out in a strained squeak. "Erin, Troy. Hi."

Monty gritted his teeth at Cindy's weak greeting, then tried to smile graciously, although he'd never felt less like smiling. Looking at Troy's expression, he had been judged, tried, and convicted on the spot. Not only was the developing relationship between himself and Cindy none of Troy's business, but after the display Troy and Erin had made on the couch a few days ago, Troy was in no position to judge. Monty also refused to be intimidated by a hostile ex-boyfriend, despite the fact that Cindy said that she and Troy were now just friends. He didn't see how any man could possibly be merely "friends" with someone as special as Cindy.

Neither of them answered Cindy's feeble greeting. She cleared her throat again. "Why don't we all go into the living room and sit down?"

Monty nodded and stood to the side to allow Erin and Troy to precede them. Although he knew he wasn't supposed to feel this way, he resented Troy and Erin's appearance.

Erin hesitated, but Troy strode inside. As Cindy turned to follow Erin, Monty tried to get her attention, but she wouldn't make eye contact.

Troy and Erin made themselves comfortable on the small love seat, so when Cindy sat on one end of the couch, Monty parked himself on the other side. The space between them stretched for miles.

Erin tried to make conversation, but Troy glowered in silence, which suited Monty just fine. Slowly, Cindy relaxed, and as she did, Monty relaxed, too, however he added little to the stilted conversation.

Cindy stood. "I think I'll go make a pot of coffee."

Monty stood before she had taken her first step. "I'll help." As he followed her into the kitchen, he couldn't help but feel Troy glaring into his back. With a quick glance over his shoulder, he returned Troy's glare to let him know he had better stay put.

Once in the kitchen, he leaned one hip into the wall as he watched Cindy make the coffee. She didn't say a word during the entire process. She measured the water carefully, adding just a bit more to the pot three times until she had precisely matched the water to the line. Then, she slowly poured the water into the machine. With the same precision, she measured the coffee into the filter before turning the switch on to brew.

Monty didn't move as he continued to watch her. She selected four brightly colored mugs, again performing each movement in slow motion. When she pulled a bag of cookies and a plate out of the cupboard, Monty couldn't stand the tension anymore.

He walked across the room to where she carefully arranged the cookies in an artful pattern and removed the bag of cookies from her reach.

"Cindy, please tell me what's wrong." He wasn't going to apologize for kissing her. It was right. If not for Erin and her boyfriend walking in on them, the timing and unexpected rightness of it would have been perfect. He wanted to kiss her again, to kiss her well and good, without interruption.

She met his eyes and took the cookie bag from his hands. "I thought you just wanted to meet me a few times, satisfy your curiosity about me, and that would be the end of it."

Monty rammed his hands into his pockets. "That's what I thought, too, but it's not enough. I want to get to know you as more than just an acquaintance."

"Well, that's not the way I wanted to get to know you."

He felt like he'd been punched in the gut. No words came.

"Monty, look at you."

Obediently, he lowered his chin to look down at himself, ran his hands down both sides of the front of his suit jacket, wiggled the knot on his tie, then returned his hands to his pockets. "What about me?" Monty considered himself a nice guy, honest, intelligent. Well dressed. Professional. A Christian.

She sighed loudly. "We come from two different worlds. We can't possibly enter into that kind of relationship."

His heart sank. Of all the things he thought about Cindy, this wasn't something he thought would concern her. The fact that it mattered to her that she'd come from a nice, normal, middle-class, Christian family while he'd been a throwaway from the wrong side of the tracks and a failure of the miseries of child welfare services stabbed his heart where he didn't think he'd heal.

Monty stiffened his back, trying to think of something to say in response without letting her know how badly she'd hurt him.

She clutched the bag of cookies to her chest like a teddy bear while the coffee maker gurgled beside her. "Look at you," she repeated. "How much did that suit cost?"

He rocked back on his heels, his hands still deep in his pants pockets, while he looked down at himself once more.

"This one? I can't remember, probably under eight hundred dollars."

"See?"

He stiffened to his full height, standing ramrod straight. "No, Cindy, I'm afraid I don't."

"If you added up the price of the suit, the silk shirt, the handpainted tie, the cufflinks, the shoes, just what you have on right now, it's probably more than the cost of my entire wardrobe!"

"So?"

She banged the bag of cookies down on the counter, catching the corner of the plate and destroying her creative placement. "Up until I got this job six months ago, I had to count every single penny. I was so broke, I made most of my clothes.

I still do. Your suit is probably worth more than my car."

"I think you're exaggerating."

"Don't bet on it."

When she made another grab for the cookie bag, Monty yanked his hands out of his pockets and grasped her wrists to hold her hands still. "Cindy, up until a few years ago, I barely had two pennies to rub together. You'll make it, too."

"No, I won't," she mumbled as she bent her head, staring at the disarray of cookies. "I don't have any marketable skills and I won't until I complete my courses, which I haven't even started yet. All I have is a rundown half a duplex that's mortgaged to the max and an old car that's coming close to its final journey to the repair shop."

"Cindy, stop it. That's not important to me. What's important to me is you."

She raised her head, and his heart nearly stopped. Her wide eyes showed such anguish, he didn't know what to do. His first impulse was to hold her close in a tight embrace, but since what started this whole fiasco in the first place was the barest start of a small kiss, he didn't know if that would make things better or worse. He didn't dare take the chance.

He gently ran his thumbs up and down her wrists a couple of times, then released her hands. "The coffee's ready. I think we'd better fix up that plate of cookies and pour the coffee, or Erin and Troy will come looking for us." What he didn't need right now was another interruption in a sensitive moment.

She nodded but didn't say a word. Monty chose to leave well enough alone.

He watched Cindy's awkward movements as she first poured the coffee, then placed the steaming cups, the cream and sugar bowls, and a small handful of spoons onto a tray that looked early-garage-sale era. Monty picked up the cookie plate and a stack of napkins and followed her into the living room.

Troy and Erin sat close together on the couch, not locked in a passionate display as he expected, but talking in hushed whispers with their heads close together. They stopped as soon as they realized Monty and Cindy had returned.

Troy leaned back on the couch, crossing his arms over his chest. "I was wondering if I should check in there to see if maybe someone had an accident or something."

Monty cringed inwardly at the word "accident" but, gathering his best business acumen, he smiled politely back at Troy, even though Troy greatly aggravated him. He could only guess at how uncomfortable Cindy felt, and he didn't want to make things any worse than they already were. Using more self-control than ever before, he held back the scathing reply that was on the tip of his tongue.

Troy opened his mouth to speak, but Erin grabbed Troy's hand and spoke first. "We went to the opening night of that new play at the Arts Club Theater. I forget the name, but it was really good. Where did you two go?"

The quick change caught Monty off guard. All he could think of was Troy being such a jerk. At a loss for words for one of the few times in his life, he turned to Cindy. Her beautiful smoky gray eyes widened, making his heart beat faster, and for a few seconds he forgot about Troy and his annoying attitude.

She then turned to face Erin. "We ended up going to this quaint little Japanese place downtown. I forget the name. We even had to take off our shoes. I'm not sure I want to know what I ate, but whatever it was, I thought it tasted very good." She turned toward him with a shy smile, then looked at Erin again. He hoped this meant she had enjoyed the quiet evening together as much as he had. "It had these neat rice paper walls, which gave it a really nice, private atmosphere around each table. You two should try it."

Troy gave a low chuckle, then turned to Cindy with a sly sneer. "Private atmosphere? In a restaurant? Oh, I get it. You didn't get *enough* privacy." He emphasized the word. "If you came here for some of that, I think it helps to close the door."

Monty gritted his teeth. He forced himself to keep silent. With a few sharp comments, he could put Troy in his place, but at what cost? Not only were Troy and Cindy friends, but they also worked together. If that wasn't enough, Troy was immersed in a serious relationship with Cindy's best friend.

Monty bit his tongue again and tried to think of an appropriate Bible verse. The best he could think of was something he'd read in Proverbs about a fool showing his annoyance, but a prudent man overlooking the insult. He planned to look it up when he got home. No matter how difficult, he determined to be prudent and honor God with his behavior and response.

Silence still hung in the room, and judging from Cindy's shocked expression, she hadn't taken the comment lightly either, which made his response even harder to withhold. Using a great deal of self-control, Monty changed the subject to something he'd read recently.

The conversation was strained and Monty hated idle chitchat at the best of times. Rather than make things worse, he decided he should leave.

To Monty's surprise and delight, Cindy not only accompanied him to the front door, but outside and to his car parked on the street.

Stars twinkled above the quiet old neighborhood, radiating a gentle charm. The sounds of traffic drifted from a main thoroughfare in the distance and a dog barked from a faraway yard. Although many houses were dark already, many living room lights remained on, with the glow of televisions indicating most people's choice of pastimes for a late Friday evening. An elderly couple stepped out of a car that had pulled into the driveway across the street, and both people waved at Cindy before they disappeared into their humble little house. The street was quiet once more.

All the tension drained from his body as he enjoyed the gentle breeze in the laid-back community.

Monty wanted a neighborhood like this. At the high-rise apartment building he lived in, no matter what hour of the day or night, people constantly milled about, hurrying to or from some activity or late-night party, especially on the weekends.

In a neighborhood of many such complexes, there was never a sense of quiet stillness, even in the middle of the night. He vaguely knew some of the people on his floor at the office tower, but he really didn't know his own neighbors at home. He recognized some, but everyone passed each other with tunnel vision, seldom acknowledging one another as they rushed by. On those rare occasions when someone did offer a greeting, they most often consisted of a quick nod without a change of pace.

Until recently, he hadn't cared. But the more he became aware of God's continuing presence in his life, the more he noticed the meaninglessness of his lifestyle. He liked Cindy's neighborhood. It suited her and seemed to give her a sense of family, and most of all, roots.

Monty and Cindy faced each other beside his car.

"I'm so sorry, Monty. I don't know what's gotten into Troy. He's really very nice and has a wonderful sense of humor, but I think he's taken on some kind of big brother role. I'm so embarrassed that he's been so nasty."

Monty had seen overprotective big brothers in a few of the foster homes he'd been placed in. Troy's behavior was far different, but if that was what Cindy chose to believe, he didn't want to burst her bubble. And now that they were no longer in Troy and Erin's company, he didn't want to discuss it.

Very gently, he cupped Cindy's smaller hands with his and ran his thumbs along the backs of her wrists. Troy and his nonsense became unimportant. "Don't worry about him. He'll get over it." He paused for a few seconds to gather his thoughts. "I wish I could see you tomorrow, but the youth group is doing *Computer Geek Day*. The last time we did this, not only did things run all afternoon, but the time kind of got away from me and we went long into the evening."

He paused, remembering the day well. The entire youth group had come to his office, where all the teens took turns at his many computers, including his personal laptop. When the parents arrived to take their kids home, many of them ended up staying, and the afternoon project had ended up lasting until late into the evening, leaving him with plenty of explaining to do to the maintenance staff the next day. He had a feeling he was in for a repeat performance tomorrow, so this time, he'd given security adequate warning.

He almost asked if Cindy would care to join him, but they'd instantly be considered a couple, and he doubted she was ready for that.

The realization struck him that he wanted to be considered that way with Cindy, and he wanted it more than anything he'd ever wanted before. Finally, he'd found the woman who saved his life. But in so doing, deep in his heart, he knew he'd also found the one woman he could share his life with, his hopes and dreams, his successes and his failures, and he wanted to be that special someone for her as well.

Was this what it was like to fall in love? Outside on the street, all thoughts of Troy and the frustrations faded into nothing as he held Cindy's hands, concentrating on her lovely face. Usually, he would be running off to tackle some unfinished project, of which he always had many, but tonight, he would have stood on the street in silence all night, just to be with her.

Without waiting for her to respond, he lifted her right hand and brushed a kiss to each fingertip. He desperately wished he could kiss her properly, but instead, he slowly lowered her hand.

She stared at him with big wide eyes, but thankfully didn't pull her hand out of his, although he purposely held her gently enough that she could have, if she wanted to. He released her before she had time to think about it.

"Good night, Monty," she stammered. "Thanks for dinner and for a wonderful evening. I guess I'll see you next Saturday when we go for that hike."

He smiled. Aside from the incident with Troy, the evening had been wonderful—one he prayed they could repeat many times.

He resisted the urge to touch her again. Nodding once, he turned to push the remote lock control on his key chain, although the thought occurred to him that in this neighborhood, he probably didn't need to lock his car. "Good night, Cindy."

Monty started his car as Cindy stood on the curb, watching him. He couldn't wait a week. If nothing else, at least he'd phone her by Wednesday, providing he could last that long without seeing her. With a little coaxing, maybe he could convince her to accompany him for lunch again. He knew his calendar was full, but something told him his schedule was about to change.

He waved once as he pulled away from the curb and drove toward home.

❧

Cindy watched as the tail lights of Monty's car got smaller and smaller. Things had not gone at all like she'd planned. Not only had she been unable to tell him that she didn't think they should see each other again, but when he tried to kiss her, if it hadn't been for Erin and Troy's sudden appearance, she would willingly have kissed him right back. Cindy thanked God they had walked in when they did, even though she'd never been so embarrassed in her life.

She didn't want to like him, but she did. Unfortunately, his feelings for her were obvious, but she knew his impressions of her were wrong. Considering the way they met and the part she had played in saving his life, she felt obligated to tell him not to trust his emotions concerning her, but she didn't know how to.

If they had met any other way, perhaps she might have given in and dated him, taking it slow and seeing what developed, but that wasn't an option. What would happen when he passed the hero-worship stage and saw her for who she really was? Unlike the sophisticated and moneyed crowd he no doubt hung around with, she was plain and ordinary, and the only reason he noticed her was that she was in the right place at the right time, placed there by God's design. His perspective of her and their relationship came from a distorted image.

She stared off into the distance at the last place Monty's car had been visible, until a barking dog brought her to her senses. Abruptly, she jogged back inside and marched up to Troy, interrupting his conversation with Erin.

Cindy wagged her finger in the air in front of his nose. "Troy Thompson, that was so rude! If you ever behave like that again, I'll. . . I'll. . ." She sucked in a deep breath. "I'll do something!"

Before he could reply, she stomped off into her bedroom and closed the door, coming just short of slamming it. He knew what she meant.

❧

Cindy pounded on the bathroom door. "Erin? Are you finished in there? I have to leave in a few minutes. I want to get a good seat."

The door opened. Erin stood in the doorway in her bathrobe, a towel wrapped around her head and a brush in her hand. "There's gotta be under a hundred people in your church. I don't think it's possible to get a bad seat."

Cindy shook her head. "You're going to be late, Erin."

Erin shrugged her shoulders and stood aside as Cindy grabbed her toothbrush. "No, I'm not. Troy's going to be here in fifteen minutes, and we'll have plenty of time. I don't know why you have to be half an hour early for your church's service."

Cindy tried to speak around the toothbrush in her mouth. "It's great that Troy is going to church with you."

"Yeah. We've talked a lot about it, and I think he's getting ready to make a commitment. We've talked a lot about things over the last few days. And we also talked a lot about you."

Cindy nearly choked on her mouthful of toothpaste water. "Me?"

"Troy doesn't trust Monty. He thinks Monty's trying to get to Robert through you."

Cindy spit. "That's ridiculous. It's just a simple crush. He'll get over it. Besides, after our hike next weekend, I won't see him again."

"I don't know about that."

The doorbell rang just as Cindy rinsed her toothbrush and dropped it into the holder. "It's Troy!" Erin shrieked. "He's early!"

Before Cindy knew what happened, Erin shoved her out of the bathroom and slammed the door shut. She didn't need lipstick anyway. "That's okay, Erin! I'll get it!" she called through the closed door. *One of these days. . .*

Cindy checked her watch as she walked through the living room. At least Troy allowed plenty of time to make a dignified arrival, although how Erin convinced Troy to go to church, she'd never know. She'd lost track of how many times she'd asked him, yet she'd never managed to talk him into going with her.

"Hi, Troy," she said as she opened the door. She decided that since it was Sunday and he was finally going to church, she would not lecture him for his rude and obnoxious behavior with Monty on Friday night. "Do you have any idea how long I've waited to see you with a. . . ," Cindy blinked rapidly at the sight that beheld her, ". . .tie. . . ?"

"Hi, Cindy."

"Hi, Monty," she squeaked out. "What are you doing here?"

"I happened to be in the neighborhood, and I was wondering if you'd like to accompany me to church this fine Sunday morning."

She happened to think otherwise. "Oh, really?"

"Yeah." He grinned. "Well, maybe I took the long way."

"And just where is this church of yours?"

His ears turned red. "Across the street from the arena."

The arena was located on the opposite end of town. Cindy backed up to let him enter, then closed the door behind him. "That's worse than the long way, Monty," she mumbled. "You'll never get there on time."

He made a great show of checking his watch, although Cindy suspected he knew exactly what time it was. "How about that. You're right. But you could always invite me to your church."

Cindy resisted the urge to groan. If he pursued his business interests with the same determination in which he pursued her, she could see why he was such a success. She could only imagine the reaction she would get from the members at her church when she showed up with a movie-star handsome man in his elegant, tailored suit, charming everyone with his fine manners and disarming smile. She wasn't sure she could handle the speculation, yet she couldn't turn him away, because if she did, he would miss church because of her. She didn't think she could handle the guilt.

At the same time, alarm bells went off in her head. If she did take him, she would lead him to falsely believe that he was succeeding and that she really was falling for him.

Cindy almost expected a bolt of lightning to materialize, despite the clear skies. She looked at Monty as he smiled at her like a hopeful puppy dog.

If she was starting to like him too much, it was only because of that, and soon, when he realized what was happening, he would be gone and never be back.

For today, she didn't have any choice but to take him to church and be gracious about it. She opened the closet door to grab the shoes that matched her skirt, then stopped with her hand in midair. Instead, she chose her flat-soled leather sandals. "Let's go," she mumbled.

eight

The words to the sermon went in one ear and out the other. If not for the notes on the back of the bulletin, Cindy would never have known the topic. She was too aware of Monty beside her to concentrate.

He sang beautifully, his baritone voice resonating in perfect pitch with every song except for one that he didn't know, and even then, he caught on quickly. Completely oblivious to the fact that no one else around them raised their hands, he closed his eyes and worshipped God freely in his own way.

When they sat for the first Scripture reading, he dutifully donned his glasses, flipped quickly to the correct chapter and verse in his beautiful leather-bound gold-embossed Bible, which was well marked with neat multicolor-coded highlighting and beautifully printed notes in the margins. Cindy opened her tattered pressed cardboard variety, complete with crumpled pages, unicolored highlighting and scribbles wherever she found room to write, and tried her best to follow along. For the length of the sermon, Monty removed his glasses, tucked his Bible under his chair, and listened with rapt attention, nodding slightly when the pastor made a good point.

He sang in harmony for the closing hymn, which Cindy knew well enough to follow the alto line. When it was finished, she noted tears in the eyes of old Mr. and Mrs. Wilkinson beside them.

As the small congregation shuffled from the sanctuary to the lobby, she tried to ignore the curious glances. She knew everyone present and dreaded the questions she would have to face next week when Monty wasn't with her.

"Your pastor is quite a dynamic speaker."

She turned her head to comment, but the exact second she

opened her mouth, the object of his observation joined them.

"Good morning, Cindy. Always a pleasure to see you. I see you brought a friend."

Cindy smiled politely. "Pastor Colin, this is. . ." She fumbled for the right words. "My friend" didn't really define what was happening between them. "This is Montgomery Smythe."

Monty smiled graciously and returned the pastor's handshake. "Please, call me Monty."

Pastor Colin nodded as they exchanged the usual pleasantries. Cindy gritted her teeth at Pastor Colin's invitation to come again, and she cringed at Monty's acceptance.

Pastor Colin's wife joined them. "We're having some people over to our home for lunch. Would you two like to come?"

They spoke at the same time.

"I don't think—" Cindy blurted out.

Monty smiled and turned to her. "I'm free for the day. What do you think, Cindy?"

Feeling like a shrew, Cindy tried to stop the rush of heat to her face. She pasted on a smile. "We'd be delighted, thank you."

The pastor and his wife left to chat with a few other people. Not wanting to arrive at their house before their hosts, Cindy had no alternative but to hang around and make small talk in the lobby. Every time someone she knew looked at her, they gave her a knowing smile. Cindy forced herself to smile back.

When only a few families remained, she led Monty outside to wait in the parking lot until Pastor Colin and his wife were ready to leave. He leaned casually against the trunk of his car, half sitting on the back bumper, enjoying the sunshine and fresh air.

At the same time that a breeze sent a ripple through his black hair, he closed his eyes, and with the smallest of smiles, he inhaled deeply. He was more handsome than any man had a right to be. She didn't know how she could ever have thought of him as a puppy dog.

He opened his eyes and smiled. "I like your church. It's homey."

"I've been coming here all my life."

"You must know everyone here quite well. It's obvious they're very fond of you."

As much as she was grateful for everyone's help and support when her grandmother died, some of the people here were too fond of her. At any given time, any number of them knew of several young men they wanted her to meet. Now that they had all seen her with Monty, if Monty really did come again, she would have to tell them something, or they would all assume the wrong thing and she'd never hear the end of the matter. She didn't need another complication. "Yes, they're all wonderful people, a little nosy, maybe, but wonderful. Oh, look, there's Pastor Colin. We can go now."

❧

The other couple invited for lunch turned out to be the elderly couple who had been beside him during the service. Pastor Colin gave thanks for their meal, and Mrs. Wilkinson immediately turned to Monty.

"You sing beautifully, Monty. I hope you are using that talent to sing for the Lord in your own church's choir."

He smiled politely. "Actually, no, I'm not in the choir. Unfortunately I have to plan my time carefully, so instead I take the youth group once every other month."

The elderly lady nodded. "It must bring back fond memories from when you were that age." She smiled, awaiting his reply.

That time in his life held few fond memories. The activities he participated in had nothing to do with church and more to do with illegal drugs. He'd been dragged to church on many Sundays, but he'd never been asked to attend a youth function. It certainly would have saved himself and a number of foster families a great deal of trial and heartache if he'd participated there, instead of getting involved in the other things he'd done.

He honestly had fun when he volunteered his time with the teens. But fun wasn't his primary reason for involving himself with the youth group. If he could spare even one teen from going through what he did as a teenager, then every minute would be well spent.

He smiled at Mrs. Wilkinson. "I never attended youth group as a teen." He slowly sipped his coffee. Even though he was new at it, he always encouraged the teens to bring a friend, especially those from a nonchurch family.

"Your church didn't have a youth group? What a shame."

Monty shook his head. She had no idea. "I became a Christian as an adult, praise the Lord."

"Really? You sang that old hymn like you'd sung it all your life."

"I've always had an aptitude for reading music, even though I don't play an instrument. It's really very mathematical."

The Wilkinsons looked at him blankly for a brief second, then turned to smile at each other. The conversation thankfully drifted on to more general topics, and with the change, he noticed Cindy beginning to relax. After Mrs. Wilkinson finished her tea, following an acceptable length of time after lunch and Mr. Wilkinson's repeated attempts to stifle a yawn, they excused themselves. Monty overheard Mrs. Wilkinson whisper to Pastor Colin that her dear husband needed his nap.

Monty wished that someday he could also experience that same mutual love and devotion. As the Wilkinsons stepped through the doorway, they exchanged hugs with Cindy. The sudden stab of loneliness surprised him.

All his life he'd managed to avoid any emotional attachment and the pain of another rejection, a lesson he taught himself after being shifted from one temporary foster home to another.

His breath caught at Cindy's smile as she waved good-bye to the Wilkinsons. He wanted to leave as well so that he could spend some time alone with Cindy, but he feared she would suggest they go their separate ways when they arrived at her home. So, when Pastor Colin offered to refill his cup, despite the fact that he'd had quite enough coffee, he accepted. They moved from the dining room to the more casual setting of the living room.

"So, Monty, I keep thinking of what you said earlier, that you became a Christian as an adult. I'm always interested in hearing such testimonies." Pastor Colin leaned back into the couch, his cup cradled in his hand, waiting.

Monty smiled his typical professional smile, but inside, his stomach tied in knots. To gloss over the story of his miserable life in the informal atmosphere of Cindy's kitchen was far different than being asked for a testimony by Cindy's pastor—in her presence. Cindy had been raised in a Christian home, while his lifestyle had been far from Christian until recently. Plain and simple, he'd been saved by grace.

"As a young child, I was shuffled through a number of foster homes in the child-welfare services system. I must admit that I wasn't an easy child to care for. A few of the families were Christians, but I rejected all they told me. In retrospect, only the grace of God got me through those years. I fell in with the wrong crowd at school and started to get into trouble, but found out quite by accident that if I spent a certain amount of time in the computer lab, I could fool everyone into believing I was there more often than I really was."

Monty paused, thinking of how he had at first only used the computer lab as an alibi. As time progressed, his interest changed from skipping school and causing trouble, to skipping classes and staying inside the school to hack away at the computer. When the teachers found out where he was and what he was doing, because he was no longer causing trouble and was actually inside the school building, they excused him more than they should have. Their leniency only encouraged him to continue skipping classes, and he tried everyone's patience by systematically calculating exactly how far he could push each individual teacher. In the end, he had been fortunate the computer had fascinated him to such a degree. He'd been one of the few in his crowd to actually graduate.

"After I graduated, I floundered for a couple of years, but when the police came around looking for a friend of mine who had some pretty heavy charges pending, I made up my mind to do something positive with myself. I eventually started my business, and although I've had my struggles, things moved along nicely until I was in an automobile accident. Once again, God sent me the message that He loved me, but this time I paid attention. My time in the hospital gave me a lot of time to think and to see how God had been with me, despite my constant rejection of Him. I made my decision to follow Jesus shortly after that." He purposely left out the fact that it had only been six months ago.

He turned toward Cindy to see her wide eyes. Many times when they were together he had wanted to tell her about her part in his decision, but every time the subject came up, she had strangely skirted the topic. This wasn't how he wanted her to find out, although he didn't understand the depth of her reaction, which didn't seem very positive.

"That's an amazing testimony. Have you shared it with your church?"

Monty politely smiled back. He would be baptized in a month, which meant sharing his testimony with the congregation then. Now that Cindy had become a part of his life, he especially wanted her to be there for him on his special day. "No, so far only with my home group, and the youth group, and of course my pastor, who was the one on duty making rounds at the hospital. I don't think the poor man had any idea that one person could ask so many questions."

Pastor Colin smiled into space, then turned back to Monty. "You'd be surprised at the questions that people ask, once they get started. It's a joy for any pastor to respond."

Monty laughed. He'd wondered if Pastor Harry had ever been tempted to sneak past his room at the hospital. Yet, he faithfully came every day, although his later visits were admittedly shorter once Monty got his new reading glasses.

"I was going to ask if you'd share your testimony, but since you haven't done so at your own church yet, I'll wait my turn."

"I'd be happy to when the time comes. I'm sure Cindy has

your phone number, and you'll be seeing me again the odd Sunday."

The pastor turned to Cindy, but spoke to Monty. "You wouldn't be taking my Cindy away from our little fellowship, would you?"

From the expression on Cindy's face, he could see they were moving too fast and her pastor had gone one step too far. He couldn't help but recall almost word for word her statement that she didn't want a romantic relationship with him. The words still hurt, but at the time they hadn't known each other long enough to make that kind of decision.

As far as he was concerned, he was finished courting her from a distance. He in no way believed in love at first sight, but he had no doubt that what he felt about Cindy was real.

"Oh, no, Cindy and I are just friends." Holding the coffee cup in one hand, he brushed the fingers of his free hand along the back of her hand and lowered his voice so only she could hear. "So far, anyway."

Cindy stood. "I really think it's time we left. Thank you so much for your hospitality, and I'll see you again next Sunday."

Monty stood as well. He could take a hint.

He shook the pastor's hand as they left. "Thank you for your hospitality. I'll see you again, soon."

৵

Cindy stared out the car window the whole way home. She'd had no idea until today that Monty only became a Christian after his accident. While she knew it was fairly common for people to come to a sudden belief in God at such a moment, the thought terrified her. Being at the point of death would change anyone. She'd also peeked at his Bible. The short time frame since he'd been a Christian explained its pristine condition. Judging from his highlighting and carefully placed notes, he had done a lot of reading in that short time. He'd also been approved by at least the pastor to take on some responsibility for the youth group.

Cindy continued to stare out the window. Could she trust

this was a firm commitment and not based on a single experience? Why did she care? As soon as they arrived back at her house, she would tell him that she couldn't see him again, including the hike, which was a bad idea anyway because she could tell that his leg still hurt.

"Cindy? Would you like to go out for dinner?"

She turned to face him, and as he smiled, Cindy's foolish heart fluttered. She did care. Against her better judgment, she actually liked the man. "I think I'd rather go home, if you don't mind."

Instead of saying good-bye from the car, he not only escorted her to the door, but before she had a chance to open her mouth, he was inside and making himself at home on her couch.

Since he was there, she made the best of it. At first they discussed the pastor's sermon, which was a good thing, since she hadn't paid enough attention. In doing so, she discovered how deeply he considered the teaching and then its practical application, and they simply just kept talking.

Before they knew it, suppertime had come and gone, so they ordered a pizza and talked some more. The depth of his research and reading was astounding, and Cindy was able to share some of the spiritual truths she'd learned over the years.

Despite the late hour, Cindy felt almost sorry when he left, which was thankfully before Troy brought Erin home.

As his car disappeared around the corner, she realized that she hadn't told him she had reconsidered the hike. More importantly, she hadn't mentioned that she thought it unwise for her to continue seeing him.

A million thoughts zinged through her head while Cindy changed into her pajamas and brushed her teeth. She tried very hard to figure out what had happened between the beginning of the day, when she dreaded Monty's arrival, and his late departure, when she was sorry to see him go.

She no longer questioned the depth of Monty's commitment. He focused single-mindedly and pursued with diligence everything he did—his faith included. They'd shared ideas and opinions, agreed on some, and disagreed on others. Best of all, he had never doted on her, nor had he indicated any other signs of hero-worship as listed in her first aid book. Everything he said and did indicated merely the beginning of a very companionable friendship, but now she wasn't as sure that she wanted only friendship.

Lying in the silent, dark bedroom, Cindy stared at the ceiling, then closed her eyes to pray for guidance. Although no answers came, she tried to be content in the knowledge that God was watching, and He was in charge.

৯৯

Monty picked up the phone, stared at it, then hung up again without dialing. Agnes rapped on his office door, dropped a letter needing his signature onto the corner of his desk, and shuffled out without a word.

He rested his elbows on the desk and buried his face in his hands. Never before had he been unable to concentrate on his work. Never. Not even when he had three projects to complete on the same day that Agnes had accidentally booked an important meeting. Now, he couldn't formulate a coherent thought.

He'd seen her just yesterday. He checked his watch. Less than twelve hours ago, in fact. Even though they'd talked for hours, they'd left so much unsaid.

Monty picked up the phone and dialed her number. Anticipating the soothing sound of her soft melodic voice, he enjoyed her calm business greeting when she answered with her official salutation as Robert's secretary.

"Hi, Cindy. It's Monty. Free for lunch?"

She hesitated a second before she spoke. "I thought you were going to stop sending me flowers."

"Well, it sure is a pleasure to hear your voice, too."

She grumbled something he couldn't quite make out and perhaps was glad he couldn't. Then she cleared her throat. "Hello, Monty, it's nice to hear from you." She paused to let out a short sigh. "The flowers?"

"I don't remember promising. You could refresh my memory at lunch."

"I. . ."

Monty smiled as her voice trailed off.

Cindy cleared her throat. "Are you sure you don't have a meeting or appointment or something?"

"Yup."

"Just a minute. I'll make sure Robert doesn't need me."

He waited patiently, tapping his fingers on the bottom of his keyboard in time with the hold music.

"Yes, I'm free for lunch."

"Great, I'll pick you up at noon. See you then."

Monty quickly postponed his lunchtime appointment, then finished his current programming project. Unfortunately, a phone call delayed his departure, making him unsure if he would be able to arrive at Cindy's office for noon. As he dashed out the door, he called to Agnes when he would be back, not giving her a chance to ask any questions. Like most days, he would stay late to catch up on the work that was starting to get a bit behind, then he'd go see Cindy again in the evening. Today was going to be a great day.

❧

Monty smiled as he hung up the phone. He knew he was pushing his luck, but after three lunch dates with Cindy this week, he noticed a change in her. Up until today, every time he'd invited her to lunch she'd been hesitant, but today, she sounded like she actually anticipated his arrival. She'd even accused him of collaborating with Robert to allow her longer lunch breaks, but he knew she was only teasing. He was making progress.

He'd almost made it out the door when Agnes stopped him. "Where are you going?" she called out just as he pulled the door handle.

"I'm going out for lunch. I'll be back at one-fifteen."

"What's that smell?" Agnes pointedly sniffed the air. One eye narrowed marginally, and she then broke out into a wide smile. "Never mind," she mumbled. "It's just the fresh gel in your hair. I see you're taking Cindy out for lunch again. Just so I can page you if I need you."

He felt his face redden. What he did with his hair was none of Agnes's business. Nor was it her business where he went, or with whom, on his personal time. Not that he'd ever taken personal time during working hours before.

He heard Agnes humming gently as the door closed behind him. He reminded himself not to let Agnes find out he was taking Cindy to the theater tomorrow night. Agnes would never let him live down his decision to start leaving on time every night.

Even though he anticipated Friday evening out with Cindy, he knew they'd have to make it an early night. Saturday was their hike, and he could hardly wait.

nine

Right on schedule at 8:00 A.M., Cindy slowed her car in front of a tall, exclusive apartment building in a neighborhood of many such buildings. With Monty's directions in her hand, she tilted her head back to gaze skyward, up the height of the building at the address he had given her. Monty's apartment was on the twenty-fifth floor.

Just as she considered searching for the visitor parking area, Monty appeared through the large glass door. Gone was the designer power suit and tie, replaced by pristine jeans and a good-quality, name-brand windbreaker, which hung open to show a colorful T-shirt. In stark contrast to the immaculate clothes, his hiking boots and baseball cap had seen better days.

As she pulled up to the curb, Monty opened the passenger door. Before he climbed in, he tossed into the backseat a backpack that was in even worse condition than her own.

"Hi."

She forced herself to mumble a hello. His familiar face grinned at her from beneath the baseball cap, but nothing else was the same. She struggled with the image.

Cindy steered into traffic. "I've been thinking. Are you sure this is wise? Have you asked your doctor about this?"

"I haven't talked to him recently, but he told me I should be getting some exercise." Out of the corner of her eye, she caught the movement of Monty resting one hand on his stomach. "I've gained quite a bit of weight due to the inactivity, so this is a good chance to start getting back in shape."

Not that she considered Monty the least bit heavy, but evidently he'd gained enough weight to buy a larger size jeans. Still, she doubted a long hike on a mountain trail was the wisest choice. Since she never got around to canceling the outing, she planned to take the easiest and shortest of the three trails and go slowly.

Soon they reached the turnoff for the park, and Cindy followed the bumpy gravel road to the parking lot. She pulled out a map of the park and traced her chosen route with one finger. "This is the one I told Erin we'd be on, in case of an emergency or something."

His smile made her heart skip a beat. "You're so sensible."

If such a comment had come from Erin, she would have taken it as sarcasm, but coming from Monty, she accepted the statement as the compliment he'd intended.

Donning their backpacks, they started down the trail, chatting about the area in general. They walked side by side and Cindy kept their pace slow. If he noticed, Monty didn't seem to mind.

She purposely stopped as often as possible, whether to watch a playful squirrel or to admire a colorful bird high on a top branch. At the sight of a nest of sparrows, Cindy pulled her camera out of her backpack. She also made Monty pose for a few snapshots, and then he took a couple of her with her own camera before they continued on the path. For awhile no words were spoken, allowing her to enjoy the wind rustling in the trees and the twittering and chattering of the birds and squirrels overhead.

Monty pushed a branch out of the way. "I love this time of year. Warm, but not too hot yet, everything is green and all the summer flowers are out." He turned to wink at her. "I know men aren't supposed to admit to liking flowers."

Cindy thought it strangely appealing that a man would not only have such thoughts, but would be able to share them without feeling self-conscious.

At some point, Monty reached for her hand and held it while they walked down the trail. Cindy didn't want to admit how much she enjoyed the small contact as they maintained a comfortable silence with their slow but steady pace.

By the time the path narrowed to a single file, they stopped to sit on a fallen tree while they had a drink of water. Cindy checked the log for creepy crawlies, then swooshed away a fly that chose that moment to buzz around her head. "I forgot to pack insect repellent. Did you bring any?"

Monty sat directly beside her. "Don't worry, I'll protect you from flying and biting monsters."

Cindy nearly choked on the water. As she sputtered and coughed, Monty patted her gently on the back. He rested his hand on her shoulder, then raised his hand to run his fingertips on her chin. "Sorry," he murmured.

Instead of replying, her words caught in her throat. Both turned at the same time, and their faces were only inches apart. Slowly, he tipped her chin up slightly, and as he tilted his head, his eyes drifted shut. Cindy couldn't help it. She also closed her eyes, and his mouth brushed hers in a slow and gentle kiss. Before she had a chance to react, he was already standing. He held his hand out to help her up, but she stood without touching him.

If she had deluded herself before, she now had no doubt where this relationship was headed, if she let it.

Since they could no longer carry on a conversation in single file, Cindy studied Monty as he walked in front of her. Due to the slightly uneven ground, she couldn't tell if his limp was worse, but she suspected it was.

Shortly after noon, they reached the halfway point and stopped for lunch. With the increase in the temperature, Cindy shed her windbreaker and tied it around her waist, and Monty stuffed his into his backpack.

Monty laid a blanket on the ground, and Cindy spread hers on top to give them a bit more protection from the hard lumpy ground. She noticed Monty wince as he lowered himself stiffly and awkwardly to sit on the blanket. She purposely didn't respond to his discomfort, taking her time to rummage through her backpack to allow him more time to get comfortable. He rubbed his leg when he thought she wasn't looking.

Cindy smiled when she discovered they had packed identical lunches—peanut butter and jam sandwiches, an apple, and juice. Monty had also brought a bag of trail mix to snack on.

Following a short but heartfelt prayer of thanks for the food and their day, they began to eat.

"This was a great idea, Cindy. I really needed this chance to get away. Too often I end up working all weekend, except for the time I take off on Sunday morning."

She turned to him as she replied. "My grandmother taught me to always have one full day off every week, a full day of rest. When she was alive, we did something special once a week, even if it was only going to the park." Cindy sighed. "I really miss her."

"That must have been nice."

"I know you said you were raised in foster homes. Didn't you ever do that kind of thing?"

He shook his head. "No. While I'm not going to say that every family that took me in was bad, I always felt like an outsider when it came to family activities. And I wasn't always the easiest child to care for. I had quite a chip on my shoulder."

"Oh, Monty, I'm so sorry. How old were you when your mother died?"

"As far as I know, she's still alive. She abandoned me when I was five."

Cindy swallowed hard. She couldn't imagine a mother simply abandoning her small child. In all likelihood, from the distorted viewpoint of a small child, he only felt he'd been abandoned, when that probably wasn't the case at all.

They made brief eye contact, and he immediately focused his attention on the toes of his boots. "Don't look at me like that," he mumbled. "She was an unfit mother. Who knows what would have happened to me in that environment. I only pray that she is safe and well and that someday she will allow God to bless her in the same ways He has blessed me."

"I'm sure she misses you."

Before she realized he'd moved, Monty grasped both her hands, riveting her attention to his face. "Cindy, she dumped me off like unwanted baggage. A couple of days before I was to start kindergarten, she took me to the mall, sat me on a bench in the middle of the food court with two plastic bags beside me, told me to stay there, and said she was getting dinner. That was the last I saw of her. When the mall closed, the security guard called the police to take me away. I was taken to a juvenile care center and then on to the first of many foster homes."

She couldn't conceive of a mother doing that, nor could she imagine the trauma to a small child. "How awful."

He stared off into space. "I know I shouldn't let it bug me, it was so long ago, but I'll never forget my first day of school. The first day of kindergarten, the other mothers hugged and cried over the other kids being dropped off, and a lot of the mothers spent most of the day in the classroom. The social worker patted me on the head, sent me in, and as soon as I was inside the classroom, she left. I felt sure that my mother would pick me up when all the other moms came, but of course, she didn't. For the longest time, I hoped she would just show up and take me home. I never saw her again."

"Are you sure nothing happened to her? She didn't have an accident or something?"

He still didn't look at her as he spoke. "No. When they looked through the bags my mother left, I remember the security guard talking to the police officer. There was a note saying my mother didn't want to be stuck with a kid anymore and not to try to look for her because she made sure they would never find her."

Cindy gulped. "Do you remember her?"

"Only through the eyes of a child. I don't even have a picture of her. My most outstanding memory is that she was always very busy, different men were always coming and going, there was a lot of smoking and drinking, and looking back as an adult, I'm sure there were illegal drugs. And we moved a lot. Often the police came, which made me even more frightened of them when they took me away from the mall. We'd just moved again when she abandoned me, so I couldn't even lead them to where I lived. They never did find her, or if they did, they've sealed the records. Obviously I've never seen my father. I don't know if she knew who he was."

"Oh, Monty. . ."

He turned to face her for a second, then turned away. "Don't feel sorry for me. God took care of me when my mother didn't. Now let's pack up and keep going."

They'd barely started again when Cindy thought she heard a phone ring. Monty halted in front of her, shucked off his backpack, and quickly dug through one of the outside pockets and pulled out his cellular phone.

Cindy tried not to let her mouth hang open as Monty opened the case and hit the button.

He shrugged his shoulders, then turned away. "Smythe Computers," he answered brusquely, then nodded a few times as he listened to the caller. He looked around, then cautiously stepped atop a fallen tree in an attempt to get better reception.

Cindy watched, dumbfounded, as Monty explained something in complicated high-tech computer lingo.

Upon completion of the call, he snapped the phone shut and eased himself down, carefully settling all his weight on his right leg. Then, he picked up his backpack, which he had left on the ground at Cindy's feet.

Cindy tapped her foot, but her thick-soled hiking boot didn't produce the desired effect, scrunching into the mulch of the trail rather than producing the more satisfying sharp staccato sound of a rap against a tile floor. She crossed her arms. "We were supposed to be communing with nature."

He grinned sheepishly. "I have my office calls forwarded to my cell phone after hours and weekends." He shrugged his shoulders, tucked the phone back into its case, and then slipped the backpack over his shoulders.

She didn't move or speak but continued to stand with her arms crossed.

"I can't expect my staff to be on call on weekends, especially when most of the time I'm at home working beside the phone, anyway."

She remembered he'd mentioned spending a lot of time working, including weekends. Up until now, though, she had no idea what that meant in practical terms. "You'd better not have a palm-size computer in there," she mumbled.

He laughed, but she noticed he didn't confirm or deny it.

Cindy led for awhile, again making sure they walked slowly and stopped often. By the time Monty took the lead once more, she noticed a significant change. He limped heavily. Although they were walking on fairly level ground, she saw traces of moisture on his brow. Of course, he said nothing.

Finally the path widened again, permitting them to walk side by side. Unlike the beginning of their journey, their conversation was stilted. She knew he wasn't out of breath, but Monty wasn't talking much. She felt an almost tangible stab into her heart, watching him try to remain cheerful, when she suspected he felt anything but.

By the time they reached the car, Monty's pace was slow and labored and his limp very pronounced. Even knowing his reaction, she had to ask, "Are you all right?"

He nodded as he tossed his backpack into the backseat, then cautiously eased himself into the passenger seat, using his arms to lower himself in, noticeably not putting any weight on his left leg. "I may have overdone it a bit, but I'm fine. Don't worry."

She worried anyway but said nothing.

Their initial plans were to go out for a greasy hamburger after their hike, but instead Cindy drove him straight home. She had to bite her lower lip and fight the tightening in her throat as she watched him pull himself out of the car.

Before he left, Monty turned and bent at the waist to lean into the car window, supporting his weight on his arms, bracing himself against the door frame. "Thanks, Cindy. We'll have to do this again. I'll be in touch." As he disappeared into his apartment building, his limp was the worst she'd ever seen.

And he never tried to kiss her good-bye.

❧

The words to Pastor Colin's sermon went in one ear and out

the other. She'd never strayed from paying attention in the past, yet it had now happened two weeks in a row, and she knew the reason. To get her mind back on track, Cindy tried reading the notes on the back of the bulletin. It didn't help.

Monty hadn't shown up at her door this morning. She'd waited for him. As the time for her to leave drew closer, she picked up the phone a dozen times, then hung up before she finished dialing his number. For the first time, Erin left before she did but thankfully said nothing. Also for the first time, she arrived only minutes before the service started and snuck into a seat in the back row.

She keenly felt Monty's absence. Even though they'd only attended church together once, she almost felt as though a part of her was missing. After the service, rather than mingling around to chat, she hurried home to check the answering machine. The display read zero.

Cindy couldn't stand it anymore. She dialed his number, but only got Monty's answering machine. Instead of telling him how worried she was, Cindy left a short, cheery message along with a request to call her back.

She stayed home, despite Erin's repeated requests to join her and Troy for the evening service. Monty didn't call.

He still hadn't called by the time she crawled into bed. Most of her prayers centered on him and waffled between prayers for healing and whatever it was that was happening between them. Cindy feared that despite her caution and careful discretion surrounding the circumstances of meeting him, it was too late. She had fallen in love with Montgomery Smythe.

ten

The intercom buzzed. "I need a coffee, please, and then I need to see you."

Cindy nearly choked on her coffee. She couldn't remember the last time Robert had said "please," which told her she wasn't going to like what he was going to ask. Cindy immediately abandoned her work to pour his coffee, then hurried into his office to find out what was wrong.

While Robert sifted through the file in front of him, Cindy discreetly checked her watch. She'd only been at work half an hour and didn't want to appear too anxious, therefore she planned to wait until nine-thirty to phone Monty at his office. The arrival of a small vase containing a red salvia, a white hyacinth, and a yellow carnation only served to make it worse, being a constant reminder of him as she watched the clock.

Robert slid the contract she had taken to Monty's office across the desk. "There's been a small amendment, and I'm going to ask you to retype the last page and take it back to Smythe Computers and have it signed again." He handed her a paper outlining the changes. "We need it right away, and I need you to witness it again and be back in time for the one o'clock meeting. And then I'll need the notes from the meeting typed, so you'll have to stay overtime."

She didn't care about the overtime. This was the chance she needed. Instead of merely phoning, she could see him in person. Cindy thanked God for His timing, grabbed the paper out of Robert's hand, and rushed back to her desk.

Fortunately, she managed to complete the corrections with little interruption. Before she ran to the elevator, she brushed her fingers over the velvety flower petals. She couldn't believe the ache in her heart after not hearing back from him.

108

Cindy drove to Monty's office as fast as she could without getting a ticket. When she entered the reception area, her heart nearly stopped. He wasn't in his office. No suit jacket hung over the back of the chair, and the desk was as neat as a pin.

She turned to Agnes. "Will Montgomery be back soon? He wasn't expecting me."

She tried not to squirm as Agnes studied her face and then the large manila envelope in her hand.

"Montgomery phoned to say he won't be in today. He said he likely wouldn't be in tomorrow, either."

Cindy's stomach tightened into a knot. She knew he never missed work unless he was so sick he couldn't drag himself out of bed.

At Cindy's silence, Agnes continued. "I wouldn't tell anyone else but you, but I'm worried about him. He didn't do any work this weekend. The few times he's phoned in sick, he'd at least done some work from home, and so far today he hasn't even answered his E-mail. In fact, he hasn't done anything all week-end. If I hadn't spoken to him personally on the phone, I'd be in a state of panic right now. It's spooky, almost like when he had his accident. You can't imagine how frantic we were at that time. He didn't show up for work. He didn't call. He didn't answer his phone. And nothing was being done from his home. It took us three days to find out what happened to him."

At least Cindy knew why he'd done nothing Saturday, but that didn't explain Sunday or today's lack of correspondence. A surge of relief passed through her, knowing Agnes had spoken to him personally.

"Did he say what was wrong?"

"Montgomery? Of course not."

She knew the woman was worried. Monty had joked about Agnes and her concern for him, but deep down, she knew he appreciated it. Cindy glanced once more at his empty office, as if she needed the reminder, then turned around. "Can I use a phone?"

Agnes's gaze wandered through the room, then settled on

Monty's office. "You might as well use Montgomery's phone. He's usually very particular about his office, but I think for you he'd make an exception."

She dialed Monty's number but only got his answering machine. When he didn't answer after she called out to him to pick it up, she phoned Robert. While she waited for him to answer, she studied Monty's office. Every paper and accessory sat in perfectly straight order. The only thing that might have been considered out of place was a pile of computer disks neatly stacked beside Monty's keyboard on the otherwise empty desk. She didn't dare touch anything, but the label caught her eye, only because it was the single thing in the office that wasn't perfect. The words "Trashing Troy" had been crossed out, and beneath that, neatly printed, were the words "Prince's Perils." She turned her head. Cindy didn't think she wanted to even guess what that was all about.

Without divulging any details, she confirmed with Robert that her errand would take longer than originally anticipated, said a quick good-bye to Agnes, and hurried back to her car. On the way to Monty's apartment, she made a quick detour at the drive-thru of the local hamburger joint. If she needed to justify herself, she could admit on the surface that she was doing this as a favor to Robert, followed by the excuse that she knew how important this business alliance was for Monty. As she got closer to Monty's apartment, she could no longer make excuses for herself. She was worried sick about him.

When she arrived at the front door, she noted that his apartment was the penthouse, which shouldn't have surprised her. She buzzed his number, but as she expected, he didn't answer.

While she fidgeted, wondering what to do, a woman exited the elevator and walked toward the door. Taking her chances, Cindy hustled inside before the woman could protest her unauthorized entry into the building.

The elevator rose quickly and silently. At the twenty-fifth floor, she stepped onto the thick red carpet and tapped lightly on his door. When he didn't respond, she tapped louder.

"Monty, open up. It's me, Cindy."

She waited, but he didn't answer.

Cindy's heart pounded as she knocked louder. "Monty, please, open the door. I know you're in there."

Silence answered her. Panic started to overtake her as she banged on the door with her fist.

She heard his voice, muffled through the door. "I'm not accepting visitors."

The door didn't open, nor did she hear movement inside. "Please. . ." Cindy rattled the doorknob. At least now she knew he hadn't died after speaking to Agnes earlier this morning. "I brought you some lunch." She hoped that perhaps food if not her presence would entice him.

Nothing. She knocked again. "Monty, open the door. I'm worried about you. I'm not leaving until you open the door, even if it means I stay here all day."

When that garnered no response, she leaned both palms against the door and spoke loudly into it. "If you don't let me in, I'm going to find the building superintendent and tell him there's an emergency, that I think you're dead or something, and he'll use the master key to let me in. I'm not kidding!"

She pressed her ear to the door, and when she heard a shuffle, she straightened and waited.

Slowly, the door opened, and Monty appeared, scowling. His usually impeccably neat hair hung in clumps, a few locks hanging over his forehead. Dark stubble shadowed his jaw, and instead of the power suit and neatly pressed shirt, he wore a wrinkled T-shirt, baggy sweat pants, and his feet were bare. Dark circles beneath his eyes contrasted the washed-out hue of his normally dark complexion.

And he was leaning on a cane.

Cindy struggled to breathe.

This was her fault. She had let her desire to spend time with him overshadow good sense.

His mouth drew into a tight line. "Yes?" he ground out between his teeth.

She tried to keep her expression blank and her attention riveted to his face instead of staring at the cane and the way he was leaning on it to support himself. She thought he'd be sore, but she hadn't expected this.

Cindy sucked in a deep breath, stiffened her posture, and held out the bag containing the hamburger and fries, keeping the envelope with Robert's contract tucked under her arm. "I brought you some lunch. And some work."

He stared at the bag in her hands.

"There's also been a slight change to Robert's contract. I know this is important to you, and he needs it back by one o'clock."

He turned around slowly, carefully supporting himself on the cane. Cindy's heart nearly wrenched in two at the pitiful sight of him. He said nothing.

Her words came out in a rough mumble. "And I was worried about you. You didn't return my calls."

Stone-faced, he glared at her in silence.

Without asking his permission to enter, she pushed the door open and squeezed past him. Being very careful not to brush against him for fear of knocking him over, she sat on his couch.

She couldn't help but notice the size and elegance of the living room or the decor. She could see her footprints in the plush of the light gray carpet, which was the same color but a few shades darker than the gray wall. The sheer draperies were the exact color as the dark burgundy couch, as was the frame on one single piece of original artwork, which hung above a pristine gas fireplace. The furniture was all of a fine quality and obviously very expensive. The decorating was sparse, but masculine and well chosen. It suited him.

The contrast between her half-duplex and Monty's apartment only accented the differences between them. His home spoke success. Hers shouted rummage sale.

She set the envelope on the coffee table and held out the bag toward him. The smell of the burger and fries wafted out. "Well? Aren't you hungry?"

≈

Monty stood and stared. He'd wrestled with the decision to call Cindy back on Sunday, but he feared she would hear the strain in his voice and ask too many questions. When she phoned an hour ago, he'd nearly picked it up, desperately needing to hear her soothing voice, but he didn't want her to feel sorry for him. Now he regretted his mistake. He'd never imagined that she would show up at his door unannounced.

He didn't want anyone to see him like this, least of all Cindy. His condition after the accident was bad enough. He'd had no control over that or his limitations during the course of his slow recovery, but his condition today was nothing short of pathetic. The surgeon had warned him about starting slowly and taking it easy. Monty knew the doctor hadn't meant it would be okay to hike the slow nature trail at the base of the mountain, but he hadn't expected the hike to affect him this severely. He'd gambled and lost, and now he was going to suffer for it, and suffer badly.

He struggled to stay standing, but the strain of leaning on the cane to support himself using the arm that had been broken was taking its toll. Before his arm gave out, mustering as much dignity as he could, he slowly made his way to the love seat across the room from Cindy and dropped himself into it.

The stiff muscles he could handle; he knew that would happen. What he had hoped wouldn't happen hit him with full force Saturday night. He woke up in a sweat after a reoccurring nightmare of the accident, only this time, when he awoke, the pain didn't disappear. He could barely move his leg without agonizing pain, and when he could grit his teeth and get beyond that, he couldn't put any weight on it without collapsing. He could barely move all day Sunday, and it wasn't much better today. Knowing his injury was self-inflicted this time made it that much worse.

He noticed Cindy avoiding his eyes as she reached inside the bag. When she looked up at him, he felt sick at her stoic expression, trying to appear unaffected at the sight of him. "Aren't you going to see what I brought?" she asked, too cheerfully.

He couldn't appear ungracious, and he was ravenous because he hadn't eaten since last night, finding it too difficult to stand to make anything and being too depressed to eat. Everything he had in the cupboard that didn't need preparation had been consumed Sunday down to the last scrape of peanut butter and the last broken cracker.

Now that he was sitting, he would have starved rather than allow Cindy to watch him struggle to get up. He sucked in his stomach in an attempt to stop the embarrassing growl of his response to the aroma of the food when Cindy sat beside him, holding the bag.

"You should eat your burger before it gets cold. This stuff is bad enough when it's warm."

He let his voice drop to a low mumble. "Thank you." Monty lowered his head as he accepted the wrapped burger and fries from her hands, not wanting to make eye contact. He closed his eyes in a short prayer of thanks for the food and ate in silence. Never had a greasy burger and lukewarm soggy fries tasted so good, and he'd never eaten anything so fast in his life, not even during his days of living on the streets.

"Would you like something to drink?"

"I don't need you to wait on me."

"Walking into the kitchen to pour a glass of milk certainly doesn't constitute waiting on you."

He flinched and leaned away as her fingers rested gently on his arm. He didn't want her sitting next to him. He hadn't showered or shaved for two days.

Monty hunched over and buried his face in his hands. "Don't touch me. Don't look at me."

"It's okay. . . ."

He shook his head, not caring that he muffled his voice by speaking into his palms. "No, it's not okay. I can't think straight from all the painkillers I've taken, yet still I can barely move. I didn't want you to see me like this. Thank you for the lunch, now please, I want you to leave."

eleven

"I'll only leave if there's someone else I can call to come help you."

Monty's heart physically ached to know that he had lost everything he had tried so hard to maintain after his accident. He had only been fooling himself. He wanted to think that after a little time all could be normal, as it was before. But that wasn't going to happen.

All he'd done was walk. They hadn't climbed anything, they hadn't exerted themselves in any way, yet the little excursion incapacitated him. He had barely held himself up at the door to talk to Cindy, and his condition had improved ten times over yesterday. Yesterday he couldn't even hold himself up with the cane. Saturday after their walk, he'd had to support himself against the wall to get to the washroom in the middle of the night, and even then, his leg had given out and he'd collapsed to the floor.

And it was all because of his own poor judgment. He'd wanted to get away from it all and spend time alone with Cindy, and in doing so he'd ignored everything he'd been told about his limitations. His disability. He had just learned the hard way what was in store for him the rest of his life.

If he couldn't take care of himself, he couldn't ask someone else to.

For the first time, he thought he'd found someone he could share his life with. Now, all his hopes for a future with Cindy vanished.

He'd worked so hard to make a good life for himself and he'd done it alone. The only friends he thought he had on the streets weren't interested in making an honest living. Everyone told him he couldn't do it, the odds were impossible, and everyone had deserted him.

When things started going well, only due to his hard work and a number of calculated risks, his former friends suddenly started showing up. When he hadn't supplied everything to make their lives easy, they'd disappeared again, and he hadn't missed them.

His new friends were few and far between. Too often, people wanted to know he was up to their social standing before they would accept him. He didn't need those kinds of friends, either.

He maintained a professionally distant relationship with his staff, but he was their boss, not their friend. It could never be any other way. He'd befriended a few people at church but hadn't had time yet to nurture a real friendship with any of them. He'd grown fond of a few of the kids in the youth group, but he was an adult and they were just kids. They looked up to him as their computer guru, and while he tried to give them whatever spiritual guidance he could, many of the kids in the youth group had been Christians longer than he had. He was the one getting the education.

He shook his head. "There's no one."

All his life, he'd had to guard himself carefully, both his meager possessions, and most of all, his heart. For the first time in his life, he started to let his guard down and allowed a chosen few people to see a bit of the real Montgomery Smythe. There were still many things he had never told anyone, not even his own pastor. Yet, he shared freely and openly with Cindy. In spite of all he told her, indications were that she liked him despite his idiosyncrasies. But now, when she saw him like this, everything he tried to do was for nothing. He'd tried so hard to show Cindy his strengths and hide his weaknesses, but he'd failed.

He didn't want her sympathy; he wanted her to love him the same way he loved her.

He kept his face covered with his hands. The stubble on his chin scraped and irritated his palms, emphasizing how miserable he knew he looked. After the hike and after a few bad cases of the sweats from the pain, he didn't want to think of how he smelled. He didn't want her near him. He wanted her to remember him at his best, cultured and dignified and proud, not the pathetic humanoid he'd become once again.

When her soft hands closed around his wrists, he flinched. Before he realized what she was going to do, she tugged his hands away from his face.

"Look at you. I never thought you'd be the type to just sit there and feel sorry for yourself."

"I'm not feeling sorry for myself."

"No?"

"No."

"What are you doing then?"

"I'm being realistic."

"Is that what you call it?"

Rather than pull his hands out of her grip, he jerked his head in the direction of the kitchen. "I can't stand long enough without falling to make myself a lousy sandwich. I made one error in judgment. One. And look what happened. Face it, I'm going to spend the rest of my life bound by limitations and leaning on a cane. Unless my arm gives out and I can't even do that anymore."

"Then hire a housekeeper or cook to help you or something."

"Never."

She shook his hands, but he pulled away from her grip as she started talking again.

"Why won't you hire a housekeeper? Are you too full of pride to admit you need the help? If you can't see past yourself, then consider this. The reason people do housekeeping is because it's a job to them. Simply said, they do it because they need the money."

Monty glared at her without commenting.

"It's not a glamorous job like yours, but it's honest work. And you want to know something? When you need the money, you'll take any honest work you can get." Cindy stopped talking for a second and abruptly poked herself in the chest a couple of times with her index finger. "I did house-keeping when times were tough because there was nothing else I could do. I considered it a blessing because it wasn't charity. Many people in my church wanted to just give me money, but instead I worked for it by scrubbing their toilets. And I did it gladly, grateful to have been given the opportunity to earn it."

He cringed at the thought of someone else cleaning his home, but to think of Cindy doing the dirty jobs nearly made him ill.

"And let me tell you this. It was exactly what I needed to get me by at the time."

"And you're trying to tell me that I should do the same for someone else. That it would have nothing to do with the fact that I am helpless and can't do it myself."

Cindy shook her head. "This is temporary, Monty. Think. Not long ago, you nearly died. When you're back on your feet, you can still use the services of a housekeeper, just to free up more of your time. There's nothing wrong with that. Give someone else a chance. You can help them, and at the same time, they'd be helping you when you need it, too. Think of what God has given you. A second chance. You're alive."

Monty stared into Cindy's eyes as he contemplated what she was asking him. During his time in the hospital, he really had been grateful for a second chance. Being so confined, he'd had lots of time to think. He couldn't do anything else.

Forced to stop and prioritize his life, he decided what was really important and what he was really aiming for. Before the accident, all he wanted was to be completely self-sufficient, never to be dependent on anyone for anything, ever again. Then, just when he could see it happening, when his goal was within reach, a random accident abruptly halted everything. Because of a special angel sent by God, he was alive, and he still didn't know why.

When he woke up after the accident, he talked to God for

the first time in his life. He asked God why He would send an angel to someone like him, even after he came to terms with the fact that it wasn't an angel who saved him, but an anonymous stranger. Because of that stranger, Monty discovered just how much God loved him. He didn't know what God had planned for his life, but Monty was determined to pay attention to God's leading. And while he was searching for God's answers, trying his best to do God's will, God placed Cindy in his path once again.

"You may be facing a few setbacks, but you have all your mental faculties. So what if you have to use a cane to walk? What difference does that really make in anything that's important? Because of God's grace, you're alive. All else is a bonus."

He stared into her eyes, her lovely gray eyes. He couldn't do anything else.

"Well?"

He'd never been so humbled in his life. She was right. He was feeling sorry for himself, and in doing so, he discounted all that God had done for him, including placing Cindy in his path once again.

His voice came out in a croak. "Cindy. . . ."

Before she could say a word, he threw his arms around her. Despite the throbbing pain in his leg as he shifted or the way every muscle in his body ached with every movement, he held her tight against him, burying his face in her hair so he wouldn't scratch her tender cheek with his rough chin. Today, she felt sorry for him, but he would pick himself up, shake the dust off his feet, and use the strength God had given him to overcome the obstacles in his path. He'd done it before; he would do it again. He would show Cindy the real Montgomery Smythe. This moment sealed in his heart the knowledge that he'd found his soul mate, that one special person he could love the way God designed.

Slowly, he could feel her arms inch around him as she returned his embrace. "Cindy, " he mumbled into her hair. "My special angel."

For a second she stiffened. "What did you say?"

"Nothing," he mumbled, shaking his head. In moving, the softness of her fragrant hair brushed against his face. She smelled like flowers. Tomorrow, he would send extra special flowers. Roses. For love. "Never mind."

Cindy stiffened in his arms, then squirmed. "Excuse me, I have to use your washroom." She glanced from side to side, then down the hall.

Monty released her and pointed. "Second door on the left." He watched her shuffle away, missing her warmth the second they separated. He'd lost his heart to a wonderful Christian woman. He prayed that one day soon, Cindy would be his lifelong partner.

Monty smiled as he heard the washroom door click closed. He wasn't going to say anything yet, not looking and feeling like this. When he could present himself properly, he would show Cindy what she meant to him. With class and dignity. And God's continued blessing.

&.

Cindy sagged against the washroom door the second she closed it behind her. He'd called her an angel. His special angel.

She caught her reflection in the mirror. Her hair was a mess, she had a zit on her chin, and a small scar beside her left eye from when she fell out of a tree trying to escape out her bedroom window as a teen. She was no angel. Cindy squeezed her eyes shut.

Snippets of conversation started falling into place. Last weekend they'd talked for hours about many things, including angels. He had briefly mentioned that at the exact moment he thought he was going to die, he heard an angel's voice and felt an angel's touch. Before she had time to think about the ramifications of that statement, he had changed to another fascinating topic, and she hadn't thought about it anymore. Now his words flashed before her like a neon sign.

She remembered praying for him just as he passed out at

the accident scene. And during the process of her first aid, her
constant checks to see if he was still breathing and that his
heartbeat remained strong, her hands had been all over him.
Was it her prayer that he thought was the voice of this angel?
She felt sick at the thought that he could be basing his
Christianity on what he thought was a vision when all it was,
was her.

She'd always wondered what it would be like to lead someone to make a decision to follow Jesus Christ as their Lord
and Savior. But not by being a supernatural being. "Nooo. . . ,"
she groaned aloud, letting her voice trail off, burying her face
in her hands.

Cindy lowered her hands slowly, dragging them down her
face until she stared at herself in the mirror once again.
Whatever Monty thought about angels, she could never live
up to such expectations.

Her mind went blank. Instead of concentrating on the problem at hand, she checked out the layout and decor of Monty's
washroom, which was as big as her bedroom. Not only did he
have a huge whirlpool tub in the corner, but also, partly
recessed in the wall in the opposite corner was an octagon
etched-glass shower stall. A pair of the biggest, fluffiest tow-
els she had ever seen hung on the wall. Like the living room,
the colors were rich and deep and just the right blends for a
perfect match.

She studied the vanity, a huge solid marble unit with double
sinks. Like his office, his home—at least what she'd seen of it
so far—was as neat as a pin and meticulously organized.
Nothing on the vanity sat out of place. A blow dryer hung
neatly on the wall and the soap dish and a toothbrush holder
were lined in perfect order. The only thing that didn't quite
belong was a familiar-looking spray decanter.

Cindy picked up the bottle. It was her favorite perfume.
First she confirmed that there was only one toothbrush in the
holder. Then, she tilted the bottle slightly to confirm that it
was nearly full. She didn't know who it could belong to other

than another woman with whom Monty would have dissolved a relationship so he could pursue her, the angel in his vision, a role she could never and would never aspire to.

Cindy forced herself to breathe. Aside from his angel delusion, he was a wonderful man, one she deeply wished she could have met another way. Knowing what she knew now, this time would definitely have to be the last time she saw him.

Cindy squeezed her eyes shut as she felt her heart break in two. Their relationship, based on the circumstances of their initial contact, had been doomed from the start. Lately, because of her own selfish desires, she'd fooled herself into believing otherwise.

She left the large washroom and walked into the living room, where she picked up the contract and sat beside him. "If I hurry, I can be on time for the meeting."

She could feel Monty staring at her as she carefully pulled the papers out of the envelope and picked through them. "Nothing has changed except the last couple of pages. Do you want to go through the whole thing or just the amendments?"

"The amendments would be fine. I trust you."

In seconds flat, she whipped a pen out of her purse and laid it, along with the new pages, on the coffee table in front of him. "I'm sure you know where to sign. I'll witness it for you."

As soon as he dutifully signed everything, Cindy stood. She plucked the pen and paper from his fingers, stuffed everything back into the envelope, and turned to the door.

"Don't get up. I'll lock the door on my way out." One last time, she had to touch him as her way of letting him know, in the only way she could, what he meant to her. Very gently, she ran her fingertips along the smooth part of his cheek. Her voice came out in a choked rasp. "Take care of yourself, Monty."

Before she changed her mind, she turned around and left.

ಬ

Monty leaned against the wall beside the entrance to his office and hung his cane over his arm in order to fish his keys out of his pocket. He probably should have given himself at least another day, but three missed days of work and a lost weekend were enough. He hadn't called Cindy since she'd seen him because he didn't want to talk to her from his bed while half stoned on painkillers. Today he had cut back, and he was going to phone her from the dignified setting of his office with a clear head.

Once inside, Monty slowly and awkwardly made his way across the room to his private office and dropped himself into his chair while he waited for the aftereffects of the exertion to pass. Today, the farthest he planned to go from his desk was the washroom. He made a mental note to cut down on his coffee consumption as he turned his computer on and waited for it to boot up.

In the silence of the empty office, Monty smirked to himself as he held up the disks for his new game, "Prince's Perils." The youth group had enjoyed it, and since its conception, he had added a number of revisions and modifications, not to mention a major name change, although he still had to admit he liked the original name. He only needed to run a few more tests, and he would be ready to register the copyright and then market the game. He patted his pocket with great satisfaction, especially considering his sour mood at his initial inspiration for the concept of the game.

Monty reached toward his filing cabinet, unconsciously using his left foot to steady himself against the chair leg as he opened the drawer. A sharp stab of pain as he pulled caused him to freeze and catch his breath. He forced himself to exhale while the pain subsided. It served as a poignant reminder to be more careful, even with these simple automatic actions.

He'd nearly forgotten what it had been like in the first month he was finally able to return to the office. This time, though, he anticipated a quicker recovery. Fortunately, today he already felt better than yesterday.

Cindy was right, he had been feeling sorry for himself. He'd almost thought he was losing it, but he'd looked up possible side effects of the medications, and one of them was depression. Now that he knew, he could deal with it.

Glasses perched on his nose, he raised his hands to the keyboard, ready to begin typing, when Agnes burst through the main door, earlier than usual, he noted. She stomped past her desk, scooped something out of her basket, and then strode straight for him. He had hoped to clear up some of the backlog before he had to deal with whatever Agnes had accumulated in his absence.

He laid his glasses on the desktop, folded his hands, and rested them on the edge of the keyboard as she barged into his office. "Good morning, Agnes. And what volume of urgent correspondence do you have for me today?"

"What are you doing here, Montgomery?"

"So glad to see you, too, and it is a good morning." He tried very hard not to laugh as Agnes's expression tightened. Where was this woman when he was growing up? He wondered about her children, and most of all, her husband, who surely had a backbone of steel. They were celebrating their anniversary soon, according to Agnes, thirty-five wonderful years, although he couldn't imagine thirty-five years with her being "wonderful."

Agnes crossed her arms, frowning at him. "Very funny."

He smiled in answer to her scowl. "I'm attempting to get caught up, Agnes. Shouldn't you be, too?"

She dropped a veritable mountain of paper on the corner of his desk. "I am caught up."

Monty lost his self-satisfied smirk and sagged, letting out a rush of air. "What's all this?"

"You left early Friday, remember. And you left on time every day of the week except one. Imagine my surprise when I discovered you hadn't done anything on the weekend. Or the last three days. And don't think I can't tell when you're here all weekend, or working at home and networking it over here."

He groaned.

She placed her palm on his computer monitor, feeling its

temperature. He'd just turned it on, so it was still cold. "You just got here. Or you would have already known what I was going to give you. Do you have any idea how far behind you're getting?"

Monty dragged one hand down his face. "I give up. Hire someone. I can start interviews immediately. Cancel my appointments for the rest of the week unless they want to come here, and make sure none of them are for lunch. Rebook the rest. I'm not leaving my office. I don't care if they say it's urgent."

"That does it. Now I know you're not supposed to be out of bed. I'm calling an ambulance."

"Agnes, I'm fine."

"No, you're not. You're. . . You're. . ." Agnes's eyes widened, and her frown was replaced by a glowing smile. She raised her palms to her cheeks. "You're in LOOOOOOVE!"

Monty buried his face in his hands. His private life was just that. Private. He was their boss, not their pal, and that meant he kept his distance, which was the way he preferred things anyway.

He raised his head and opened his mouth, but Agnes beat him to it.

"It's about time." She wagged one finger in the air.

"Don't you have some work to do?"

She shook her head. "It's all done. And sitting on the corner of *your* desk."

"Agnes, you're fired."

As usual, Agnes ignored him. She patted the top of the pile, then dutifully straightened it, matching up the papers to form a perfect stack. "The courier will be here in two hours for these letters."

He sighed loudly, welcoming the change of topic. "They'll be ready, Agnes."

"And don't forget your appointment with Dennis Bancroft. He'll be here at ten o'clock. I heard he recently got married." She sighed airily.

Monty ignored her not-so-subtle hint. Besides, the idea of getting married now appealed to him like never before. "Thank you, Agnes."

"Let me remind you that the Carolina project is due in three days. I've ordered another case of blanks for tomorrow and I placed another order with the printer for the instruction manuals. The latest figures indicate it's another winner. I knew it would be."

"Thank you, Agnes."

"And if you want my opinion on the Debonair contract. . ."

Monty couldn't stand it anymore. He opened his mouth to tell her he knew exactly what was lined up, but she beat him to the draw again.

"Never mind. I'll send you an E-mail."

He glanced at her desk across the room. He didn't doubt that she would.

Agnes patted the pile of paperwork once more, turned, and left. Despite her sharp tongue and questionable respect for his position, Monty appreciated her from the depths of his heart. She had proven herself to be an invaluable asset to both the company and to him personally. He made himself a note to give her a gift on her anniversary and began signing the letters.

He managed to work without interruption all morning, except for the few minutes he set aside every day to phone the florist.

Knowing he wasn't going to be mobile enough to take Cindy out for lunch made him miss her even more. He'd taken her out almost every day last week, a habit he could quickly get used to. If he closed his eyes, he could picture her smile. Monty picked up the phone and dialed Circuits, Inc.

twelve

Cindy ran her fingers on the velvety petals and inhaled the heady fragrance of the latest bouquet. This time it was three roses, red, yellow, and white. The very first bouquet he had sent was a dozen roses. She hadn't thought twice about it then, other than to admire their simple beauty. This time the thought terrified her. Roses were the flowers of love.

Rather than dwell on it, she convinced herself that the florist had simply run out of different variations; after all, by now Monty surely had used up all combinations of flowers in his chosen pattern of colors.

No matter how hard she tried to concentrate, she couldn't get Monty out of her head. Despite her best efforts to submerge herself in her job, every time she moved, their heady aroma drifted toward her, teasing her, reminding her of him. She placed the flowers on the farthest corner of her desk, but it didn't help. As the temperature rose outside, the air-conditioning kicked on, blowing the fragrance on her anyway.

Cindy couldn't stand it. She was about to give them to one of the secretaries when the phone rang.

"Hi, Cindy," a flowing deep voice purred over the phone. "Busy for lunch?"

Just what she didn't need today. "Hello, Glen. I'll see if Robert is free."

Without giving him a chance to respond, she hit the hold button and buzzed Robert's office. Before she replaced the handset, the second line lit up.

"Hi, Cindy. I miss you."

A shiver ran through her, but she didn't know if it was anticipation or a bad case of nerves. "Hi, Monty. Robert's line is busy. Would you like to hold?"

"I'm not calling for Robert. I want to talk to you."

Her heart pounded and she willed her hands to stop shaking, but they couldn't, so she held onto the phone with both hands for dear life, swiveling in the chair so the other secretaries couldn't watch her as she spoke. "Sounds like you're feeling better. How are you? I guess you're calling from the office."

"Yes, I'm feeling much better. I'd really like to take you out for lunch, but I'm confining myself to my office at least until the end of the week. Would you like to pick something up and join me here? Or I can have something delivered, whichever you prefer."

"I think I'd prefer to. . ." She swallowed a breath of air. "I'm really too busy. I'm going to work through lunch."

"Oh."

He sounded so disappointed she almost gave in. "I'm sorry, but I have to go now. I'll catch you another time, okay?"

"Oh. Okay. Well, another time.. Bye, Cindy."

She mumbled a quick good-bye and hung up the phone. She felt like a heel.

By the time lunch rolled around, Cindy's stomach rumbled. To make matters worse, she'd been so distracted when she left the house that she'd forgotten her lunch on the counter.

She hadn't lied. She really was busy, although not so busy that she was required to work through lunch break. However, rather than make a liar out of herself, she ran across the street to the deli for a sandwich, intending to run back and eat it at her desk while she worked. As she stood in line, Troy appeared beside her.

"Buying a sub at the lowly local deli?" He glanced behind them at the growing line, then back to her. "Not going out with Mr. Upwardly Mobile today?"

"Troy, stop it."

They stepped forward as the line moved. "So, is this thing with him serious?"

"Thing?" Cindy cringed. The word made the relationship

sound cheap and tawdry. Monty's intentions were nothing but honorable, however misplaced. She'd never met anyone like him before and likely never would again. The "thing" between them would have been perfect, if not for his angel delusions.

"I don't know," she replied, not knowing what to say to Troy. Not that it mattered. The "thing" was now over.

"I'll bet you're wondering why I'm asking."

Cindy didn't think she wanted to hear it, but she could no longer handle Troy's animosity toward Monty. Monty may have been living in a fantasy about her, but he didn't deserve the way Troy was treating him. "Not really. But you're probably going to tell me anyway."

He glanced from side to side, then back to Cindy. "I'm only saying this as a friend." He paused as they stepped forward in the line. They were next.

"Go ahead," she said, narrowing her eyes.

Troy hunched his shoulders to minimize his height. After spending so much time with Monty, looking eye to eye with him, she wasn't used to Troy's height anymore. The thought scared her.

"What do you know about him? Are you sure he's not just using you?"

"Using me?"

"You know, to get to Blackmore through you. Blackmore is a very powerful entity in the business world, and whoever gets that contract stands to make a small fortune. Monty isn't the type you'd usually go out with, nor do you seem the type he'd have in his regular social circles."

Cindy would have laughed if Troy hadn't been so serious. She really didn't go out with anybody, and the last person she'd been out with was Troy, and that only on a friendly basis. If anyone wasn't her type, it was Troy. "Nothing like the type I usually go out with? And what type do I go out with? You mean he's nothing like you."

The person in front of them stepped away. They cut their

conversation off abruptly as they placed their orders, then waited for the clerk to assemble the submarine sandwiches, giving Cindy time to think without Troy talking.

Troy hadn't seen Monty the way she had. The first time he'd walked into the office to see Robert, she'd never in her life seen anyone so shaken. And now that she knew Monty, she knew how hard he must have been trying to keep his image dignified and professional. She wished she knew if it was the simple shock of seeing someone he'd never expected to ever meet or seeing his special angel at work at a very mortal job.

The opposite of Troy's suspicions, Monty didn't need her to win favor with Robert. It was the other way around. Robert constantly told her how much he trusted and respected Monty, what an asset their association would be, and then proceeded to tell her how compatible she'd be with Monty. If she questioned anyone's motives, it would be Robert's. He'd delivered her right into Monty's lap, hand-carrying the contract twice.

Every time she thought of Monty, she dearly wished they could have met another way, although it was pointless to pray for a past that could not be changed.

Troy's voice startled Cindy back to the present.

"I'm paying for both of those," he said to the clerk as he pulled his wallet out of his back pocket. He handed Cindy the bag containing her sandwich, she mumbled a thank-you, and they walked back across the street together.

"Now, where were we?" he asked as he opened the main door for her.

"You were telling me the type of man I go out with, I do believe." Cindy couldn't help her scathing tone and hoped Troy could tell how annoyed she was with his insinuation.

"Why do I get the feeling you think I'm wrong?"

"I don't just think you're wrong, Troy. I know you're wrong."

"How do you know his intentions are honorable?"

Of that she had no doubt. The only thing she couldn't be

sure of was the reality of his perception of her as an ordinary and very human person. "He's honorable."

"I still think he's putting the moves on you to gain favor with Blackmore."

Cindy couldn't stand it anymore. Not that she owed Troy an explanation, but his mistrust of Monty cut her to the core. "Remember last fall, that bad car accident on the way home from first aid practice?"

Troy nodded.

Her voice dropped to a hoarse croak. It was a night she would never forget for the rest of her life. "The injured man was Monty. When he came to see Robert to discuss that contract, he recognized me."

The elevator door opened and Cindy hustled in. She turned as the door swooshed closed, just in time to see Troy standing with his mouth open, but no sound coming out.

❧

Cindy smiled at the delivery man, then set the latest vase of flowers on the corner of her desk. This time, she had no idea what the exotic variety was called, but they were beautiful, fragrant, and probably outrageously expensive. And they were red and white and yellow.

Her heart ached as she inhaled their sweet perfume. She hadn't seen Monty for nearly a week. He'd called her a few times at work, but she'd been able to get off the phone quickly, knowing how much respect Monty held for the sanctity of company time.

When Monty called her last night at home, she'd almost been rude to him. She contributed very little to the conversation, then claimed she planned to go to bed early. Instead of sleeping, she stared at the ceiling most of the night.

She couldn't continue this way. It was too hard on both of them.

If she continued to see him, the day would soon come for her to fall off the high pedestal Monty unwittingly placed her on, and when that happened, she wouldn't be able to bear his disappointment. Yet, she couldn't continue to avoid him without making a clean break. She missed him so much her heart felt like it was already broken. She didn't know which was worse.

Rather than dwell on it, Cindy busied herself with the ever-growing pile of correspondence on her desk. Almost ready to hit the print button, out of the corner of her eye she saw a tall man in a dark suit striding toward Robert's office door.

She squeezed her eyes shut. Glen Evans. Just the person she didn't need to see today.

In a flash she stepped in front of Robert's door, blocking the entrance. "Hello, Glen. Do you have an appointment?" she asked, knowing he didn't.

"He'll see me."

Cindy counted to ten in her head and looked up at Glen, who was as tall as Troy. "Please have a seat and I'll buzz him first." Glen knew the routine, so she didn't know why he still played these power games.

She waited for him to sit before she told Robert he was there.

With her hands folded on the desk, she stiffened her back and did her best to smile politely. "Mr. Blackmore requests that you come back in fifteen minutes."

Glen glared at her. "I have nowhere to go for fifteen minutes. I'll wait here." Glen crossed his long legs and smiled at her, inviting her to carry on a conversation.

"There are some magazines over there." Cindy returned his smile, then nearly fainted when she looked at the table. Except for the "Thank You For Not Smoking" sign she'd put there for Robert, her whole pile was gone except for one old Christmas issue of a women's magazine, making her wonder where her stockpile had disappeared. If she found them in the lunchroom, she just might scream.

"I guess I'll just have to sit here and watch you work." He never lost his insipid grin.

Cindy tried her best, but she couldn't type with him watching her like a hawk. Finally, she held her hands in midair above her computer and glowered at him. All he did was flash a dashing smile at her.

"Do you mind?" she asked, trying not to sound as annoyed as she felt.

"Not at all. I like watching you." His smile widened.

Cindy's hands landed palms down on the desktop. "If you're that desperate, maybe I've got a book in my purse you can browse through."

He leaned forward. "What kind of book?" he whispered suggestively.

Cindy ground her teeth as she searched through her purse. "Actually, all I've got is my pocket Bible. It has real small print, but it's full of great reading material."

Glen's little smirk dropped, then resumed. He must have thought she was kidding, but she wasn't. He leaned back in the chair, twining his fingers behind his head. "No thanks, I'd rather watch you."

Although she couldn't really spare the time, she gave up and chatted with him until Robert buzzed.

On his way out, Glen smiled and winked at her. It was the last thing she felt like doing, but to be polite, she smiled back and resumed her typing.

All day long, Robert continued to give her projects faster than she could complete them. With only an hour left in the day, Robert appeared again to drop yet another project into her *in* basket.

"I know you've been working extra hard, Cindy, but I need this finished tonight. I realize today is Friday, but I need this for an early meeting on Saturday. I already owe you a lot of time off, but would you mind working late tonight?"

Cindy shook her head and set her project aside. "Don't worry about it." Since it was Friday, she expected Monty to call about plans for the weekend. This way, she had a legitimate excuse not to talk to him. Her throat constricted and she blinked away a burning at the back of her eyes. One day soon,

Monty would give up and she would never see him again. Wasn't that what she wanted?

❧

Monty sat in his office with the door closed, not removing his hand from the phone after hanging up, and stared at the blank wall.

Earlier in the week he'd had his suspicions but had chosen to believe her when she said she was too busy to talk. Last night she'd claimed to be too tired. He knew she wouldn't lie about having to work overtime, but she had also said no to seeing him on Saturday. When she said she couldn't accompany him to church on Sunday, he could no longer fool himself. She was avoiding him.

He had been so sure she felt the same way about him that he felt about her. Every time they were together, every time he talked to her, he knew without a doubt that Cindy was the woman God had set aside for him.

He closed his eyes, thinking about their walk in the woods, before the pain in his leg had killed the day. He'd kissed her, and although the moment was brief, she'd responded. He'd held her hand and she hadn't pulled away. He couldn't possibly misinterpret those things as the signs of a blossoming relationship.

Since then, he'd imagined a future married to Cindy. He thought about family life and performing normal household chores. He didn't know if he'd ever be able to maintain his balance enough to stand on a ladder. Running to play with children would be out of the question. He knew he wouldn't always be able to walk unassisted.

But those things were minor in God's big picture. Cindy was right. Feeling sorry for himself was wrong. God had truly given him a second chance and commissioned him to make the most of what he had.

The phone rang, bringing Monty's attention back to where it should have been in the first place, on his work. He'd been staring off into space so long that the screen saver had come on.

The caller was Robert Blackmore, asking a simple question.

Monty grinned. He purposely made a mountain out of a molehill with Robert's simple question and left the poor man with more questions than when he first called. Then, he graciously volunteered to assist Robert with the solution in person.

As he hung up, he dropped his half-eaten sandwich into the wastepaper basket, pushed all his uncompleted work into the top drawer, and slammed it shut.

He painfully made his way across the office, not stopping to talk to Agnes on his way out. "I'm gone until Monday," he called over his shoulder as the door closed behind him.

Using every ounce of self-control, Monty barely managed to contain his impatience as he inched through the growing rush-hour traffic. He arrived as the staff members were starting to leave, making him wish he could run, desperately hoping and praying he could still catch Cindy before she left for the day.

Alone in the elevator on the way up, Monty leaned against the wall with his cane crooked over his arm to make one last check that his tie was straight and his hair was neatly in place.

Except for the cane, which he couldn't control, he was ready.

The four older secretaries stood together in front of the elevator when the door swooshed open. They stopped their chattering and stared at him, then stepped back to allow him to exit. Their surprise at seeing anyone coming in at the close of the day was more than obvious.

He hobbled stiffly, trying his best to keep his pace with the cane even, until he stood in front of Cindy's desk. She raised her eyes to see who was standing in front of her desk. When she saw him, she fumbled and dropped her pen.

"Monty! What are you doing here?" She scrambled to catch her pen before it rolled off the desk.

"I've got an appointment with Robert, but I'd like to see you first," he said, grateful for the emptiness of the large room. "I've felt like you've been avoiding me, Cindy."

"Well, I. . ." She bit her bottom lip before her eyes lowered, and she stared intently at the pen in her hand.

Monty cringed at the squeak of a door opening. "Montgomery. So glad you could come on short notice. Please, come right in."

Five minutes. If he could only have five minutes alone with Cindy. He faced her, hoping his eyes could show the pleading of his heart. "Please, Cindy, I have to talk to you. I have to know if I've done something wrong."

Cindy's face paled. "You'd better go in now. I have a lot of work to do."

He hoped that she meant she would still be there when he got out of his meeting with Robert, but somehow he doubted it. Following Robert's request, he took a seat in his office and covered everything as quickly and efficiently as he could, trying his best to hurry yet not be rude. They were nearly done when Robert's phone rang.

Robert's brows knotted as he listened to the caller. "What do you mean, everyone's gone?" He paused for a few seconds to look at his wristwatch. "Surely you can find somebody." He frowned as he listened, then opened his eyes wide and turned his head to stare at Cindy through his office window.

"What do you mean, Cindy? Is this some kind of joke, Thompson?" His eyes narrowed. Robert crooked the phone on his shoulder and crossed his arms as he continued to listen to the caller.

Monty's mind raced. Thompson. The name was familiar, but he couldn't place it. Most of all, he wanted to know what this had to do with Cindy.

thirteen

Robert hung up the phone. "I just received a phone call from the supervisor of our assembly department. Seems like we've run into a problem that I have to deal with immediately. Please excuse me." With a nod of his head, Robert rose, then stepped outside his office to stand in front of Cindy, who was still working diligently at her desk.

Assembly department. Supervisor. Thompson. . . A light-bulb went on inside Monty's head. Troy Thompson.

Monty's gut clenched. He didn't know what happened, but apparently someone was in serious trouble, and somehow Cindy was involved. If she faced disciplinary action or worse, termination, even if it cost him the contract, he would offer her a job working for him and leave with her. He still hadn't found a suitable applicant for the position he'd advertised for, and he had no doubt that with a little training, she was more than capable of doing anything she set her mind to.

He struggled to his feet and stood half leaning on the cane and half on the door frame, watching helplessly.

Cindy glanced from side to side, then briefly at Robert as he stood in front of her desk. "Yes, Robert?" she mumbled as she continued to type.

"I just spoke to Troy Thompson."

Her brows knotted as she stopped working. "Troy? He's still here? What does he want?"

"He just told me everyone down there has gone home, including Norburn."

Cindy laid her pen down and shrugged her shoulders. "So?"

Robert cleared his throat. "Thompson saw your car in the parking lot, so he knew you were still here. Our big order for Scheulers didn't get out. The truck is here now, and we need you to load it."

Monty blinked. Did he hear that right?

Cindy's mouth opened, then snapped shut. "But I. . ." Her voice trailed off. "It's been a long time, Robert."

Robert paused to run his hand over his balding head, then shoved his hands into his pockets. "It appears I owe you an apology. I remember once you told me you'd been a forklift operator, and I didn't take you seriously. Now I do."

She sighed and hit the save key on her computer. "All right," she mumbled as she rose from her chair. "Let's go."

Rather than sit alone in Robert's office, Monty took advantage of the confusion and accompanied Robert and Cindy into the elevator and down to the shipping area on the ground level in the rear of the building. Fortunately, they walked slowly for him.

Next to a large, open, warehouse door, Troy stood alongside a very annoyed truck driver.

Cindy's high heels clicked on the cement floor as she approached Troy. She placed her hands on her hips and glared up at him. "Don't tell me you can't do this, Troy."

Troy shrugged his shoulders and raised his palms in the air in defeat. "Honest, I've never driven one, and I didn't figure this would be a great day to start."

Cindy mumbled something under her breath, then removed the paperwork from Troy's hand.

Troy pointed to an area of the warehouse. "All we need is for you to load it. I already checked it twice, just like Santa."

"Just like Santa. . ." Her voice trailed off.

Troy shrugged his shoulders again. "Ho, ho, ho," he said lamely.

Cindy hopped up onto the forklift, which was parked neatly against the wall, tucked her skirt beneath her, then started the motor. Her hair streamed back as she drove, her full skirt flowed around the seat, and even wearing high heels, she worked the pedals with ease.

Monty watched intently as she drove through the warehouse,

likewise Robert, Troy, and the truck driver. First she headed toward two pallets stowed in the loading bay. Maneuvering the forks underneath the pallet, she threw the levers into place, lifted the stock, and slowly drove the forklift in reverse to the trailer parked in the loading door. Efficiently, she spun the forklift around and inched forward, poking her head out to the side to see where she was going from behind the merchandise. The hydraulic lifters reverberated, followed by the revving of the forklift motor. The trailer shook with a slight bump as she pushed the load into place.

Driving in reverse on the forklift, she exited the trailer and headed back into the warehouse for more product.

"No one in accounting is going to believe this," Robert mumbled to no one in particular.

Troy nodded but said nothing.

Monty hung his cane on his arm, leaned against the wall, and watched Cindy handle the forklift expertly, his attention riveted. Upon completion of her task, she returned the forklift to the designated area and passed the copies of the bill of lading to the truck driver to sign. When the paperwork was done, he drove away.

They rode up the elevator in uncomfortable silence. Robert briefly thanked Cindy, but Cindy only mumbled a response and stared intently at the button panel. Monty didn't dare say anything, because by all rights, he shouldn't have been there in the first place.

Cindy continued her work without saying a word, and Monty followed Robert back into his office, where they completed the final details of his alleged reason for coming. Fortunately, Cindy had not yet completed her task, allowing Monty the opportunity he sought.

Taking a guess that Robert would stay until Cindy was finished, Monty remained in Robert's office making small talk, although he hated aimless chitchat. By the time Cindy rapped on the door, he'd had more than enough meaningless chatter.

Her movements were stiff and abrupt as she waited for

Robert's final signatures, then left Robert's office. He excused himself and made his way to her desk to witness her ramming everything haphazardly into the drawers and slamming them shut.

"Hi," he said, as if she didn't know he was there.

"Hi," she mumbled back as she grabbed her purse.

"Got plans?"

"Uh, well, sort of, I don't know, uh, not really. No." Her voice dropped to a mumble. "But I'm really tired, and I want to go to bed early."

"If you're tired, I'd like to treat you to dinner. It's late, and you must be starving. This way you won't have to cook or clean up."

He forced himself to smile and then spoke before she had the chance to turn him down. "I want to know why you've been avoiding me. I promise if you don't want to see me again, I won't bother you after today, but I have to know."

"It's nothing you've done. It's just that. . .well. . ."

Monty couldn't stand it anymore. He gently grabbed her hand to stop her from fumbling with everything she could possibly lay her hands on. "Please, Cindy. I don't want it to end this way."

She stared down at his hand holding hers, then up to his face and past his shoulder, where he knew Robert was surely watching, but he didn't care.

"All right. But I'd rather not go out. I'd rather go home and order pizza or something."

As long as it was an invitation, he didn't care where they went or what they ate, and the privacy of her home was by far the best setting.

He gave her hand a gentle squeeze. "Sure. I'll meet you there."

❧

Cindy's hands shook so hard she could barely get a proper grip on the steering wheel. She nearly dropped her house key when she let herself in. No sooner had she opened the door, when the low hum of Monty's car sounded from the street, then went silent.

The entire drive home she hadn't been able to think. Her mind was still completely blank. She had no idea what she would say to him.

Monty's flowing baritone voice sounded from behind her. "Hi."

"You made it." Cindy smiled inanely. If she came up with any more equally intelligent statements, he wouldn't want to see her again anyway.

"Yeah."

Since he was leaning heavily on the cane for support, she moved out of the way to let him pass first. However, instead of continuing into the living room, he deposited the cane behind him and leaned one hip against the wall as he cupped her chin with both hands, forcing eye contact. She couldn't have looked away had she wanted to. His dark brown eyes radiated what she could only think of as sadness and regret.

Monty's voice came out low and raspy, doing strange things to her insides. "I was going to ask if you wanted to eat first or talk first, but you're so jumpy, I think we should just get it over with. What do you think?"

Cindy nodded dumbly. His hands were warm and his touch tender and gentle as he brushed her cheeks with the pads of his thumbs. She couldn't help herself as her eyes drifted shut and she let herself sag. His hands drifted down from her cheeks to her shoulders, and she allowed him to pull her closer until they were pressed close together and his arms locked around her. Briefly it registered that he was no longer leaning on the wall, but his unsteady stance indicated he was only standing unsupported by balancing most of his weight on one leg. With this in mind, Cindy slipped her hands to his waist, then up his back to hold him tighter, trying to tell herself that she was only helping to support him.

As she did so, he brushed his mouth against her cheek, then her ear, then buried his face in her hair. She nearly melted at the intimate contact.

She needed this moment, the first time he'd held her as she needed him to hold her, but this must also be the last time. She tried to burn into her memory everything about him. His touch. His strength. His gentleness. The almost desperate way he clung to her. She wanted to remember this moment forever.

Yet, no matter how much she enjoyed his touch, as if she hadn't already given him the wrong idea by returning his embrace, Cindy knew she had to tell him quickly what she had to say, while she still had the strength to do so.

He didn't release her as she started to speak. "I can't see you again," she whispered.

He stiffened, then tightened his embrace. "Why not?" He nuzzled into her hair.

The man didn't play fair. "I'm no angel, Monty."

"I know you're not."

She could feel him trailing light kisses along the crook of her neck. She started to tremble. "No, you don't understand. Not in the endearment way. I mean I'm not a real angel. I'm not even close."

"I know that. You're not a man." He brushed his lips against her throat, then his warm, moist kisses moved upward to her ear as his hands caressed her back.

Cindy thought her knees would give out. She was trying to tell him something, and he was getting her all confused. It was coming out all wrong. "A. . . a. . .man?" she mumbled.

"Angels always appear as men. At least they do in the Bible."

She couldn't think with him nibbling on her ear. "That's not what I meant."

His soft chuckle banished the last semicoherent thought she had. "Okay," he mumbled in her ear.

She couldn't have opened her eyes if her life depended on it. "I mean I'm nowhere close to an angel in any way."

"Good, because I'm going to kiss you now as a woman, the way I've wanted to kiss you for a long time." His mouth moved slowly from her ear to her cheek, nibbling short kisses. By the time his mouth reached hers, her lips were parted and waiting. He gave her the sweetest kiss she could ever hope for, loving, tender, and passionate at the same time. And she returned his kiss with all the love in her heart.

Slowly, he pulled away just a little, then started to speak with his lips still brushing hers. "Cindy, I—"

Outside a car door slammed, then another. Erin's screech was followed by Troy's playful growl, and Cindy could hear footsteps running up the stairs.

Monty mumbled something under his breath she wasn't sure she wanted to hear. Then, he pulled back. "History repeats itself," he grumbled as he used both hands to swipe his hair back. He started to straighten his tie just as Erin burst through the door.

Erin's feet skidded to a halt. "Cindy. Monty. We didn't know you'd be here."

Cindy drew in a deep, composing breath. "We didn't know you'd be here, either, so we're even."

Troy showed up behind Erin, then he also stopped dead in his tracks. He looked down at Monty leaning on the cane but said nothing. Cindy narrowed her eyes and glared at him as a warning to behave more civilly to Monty than the last time their paths crossed. "We were about to order pizza for dinner. Care to join us?"

Troy smiled. "Sure, we haven't eaten yet either. Sounds like a good idea."

She walked into the living room with Monty close behind. "I hope you don't mind," she whispered over her shoulder.

"No, I don't mind," he said, but he sighed like he did.

She knew she was stalling, but since he had gotten her so rattled, she needed more time to explain herself. She hadn't exactly done a good job on her first attempt.

Troy and Erin got comfy on the love seat, but when Cindy sat on the large couch, instead of sitting on the other end, Monty sat beside her, then grasped her hand. She felt the heat rise on her face, but rather than make a scene in front of Erin and Troy, she didn't protest.

"Norburn owes you a big one, Cindy," Troy said, thankfully breaking the awkward silence. "You really saved his bacon today."

"I guess."

"Sorry to do that to you with no warning, but I didn't have any other option."

"I know."

Monty gave her hand another gentle squeeze. "You drove that forklift like an expert. I was impressed."

The heat in her face rose again. "Thank you, but it's been awhile since I've done it, obviously. So, what kind of pizza does everyone want?"

After the pizza was ordered, the conversation turned to general conversation and more of Erin's bad jokes, giving Cindy a chance to regroup her thoughts. Monty insisted on paying when it arrived, which prompted Troy to say that next time was his turn. Although unexpected, Cindy enjoyed the new, more pleasant interaction between the two of them.

Like typical men, their conversation drifted to work, and when Monty mentioned that his latest computer game was selling well, Troy's face lit up like a Christmas tree.

"Games? You make computer games? What kind of games? Got any on you?"

She felt Monty flinch. He didn't let go of her hand, but patted his breast pocket with the other. "Well, I do, but it's a beta version. I have a few more tests and trials to run and a few more revisions to do before I can market it."

"I can test it for you on Erin's computer."

Erin poked Troy in the ribs, but Troy ignored her. Monty turned to Cindy as if asking permission. Cindy shrugged her shoulders. She had no idea if Monty could fixate on a game like she knew Troy could, but if nothing else, she was relieved to see the two men getting along for a change. Not that it mattered. Soon the only time she would see Monty would be when he came to see Robert.

Monty pulled a pile of disks out of his pocket. "It's called 'Prince's Perils.' I guess I can install it for you."

Cindy knotted her brows as she tried to think. She didn't know anything about computer games, but she remembered hearing that name before.

Troy bolted into the den while Monty made his way more slowly. He installed the game for Troy while explaining the general theme. The Prince had to win many battles against the Evil Overlord, each level becoming more difficult, in order to save the Princess, who was being kept prisoner. After setting the options menu, he returned his glasses to his pocket and pushed himself up to trade places with Troy.

All Troy's attention focused intently on the game as he started to play. Cindy took the opportunity to lean forward and get a closer look at the characters. The dark-haired handsome prince was considerably shorter than the tall blond evil villain, and she imagined it to be somewhat like a medieval David and Goliath. She watched the back of Troy's blond head, then glanced beside her to Monty's nearly black hair. Standing next to Monty, at eye level, she calculated the height difference between Monty and Troy.

Then it came to her. On the day she used his phone when he wasn't in his office, he had a pile of disks sitting on his desk. The words "Trashing Troy" had been crossed out, and the new title, "Prince's Perils" had been neatly printed beneath.

"Monty!" she whispered in his ear as she watched Troy blow himself up onscreen. "What have you done!?"

"I couldn't help myself," he whispered back as he again grasped her hand. "It came to me in a stroke of genius."

Troy once more did battle with himself. This level of the contest saw the evil villain eaten by a fire-breathing monster. Troy bit the big one, again.

"I kinda like it," Monty whispered. "You must admit, it gets you right here." He raised his free hand to press his loosely closed fist against his heart. "Wait till you see the Princess." He quirked one eyebrow.

Cindy wasn't sure she wanted to know. "How long does this go on?"

Monty checked his watch. "That depends. He seems pretty good at these games, although he's got the trial version, and I set it to the lowest degree of difficulty."

"Don't I get a turn?" Erin whined. "It's my computer."

In changing places, they missed a window of opportunity, making "Prince Monty" lose a little ground, which Cindy thought rather poetic justice.

Cindy didn't want to watch Erin take a turn at blowing up the onscreen Troy. "I'm going back to the living room. Anyone care to join me?" Both Troy and Erin shook their heads, then squealed with glee as the onscreen Evil Troy disappeared over the edge of a cliff, accompanied by an echoing thud. Cindy gave Monty's hand a gentle tug to pointedly encourage him to leave the room.

As they sat side by side on the couch, Monty attempted to grasp both her hands in his. She yanked her hands away and shuffled a few inches away from him. "Don't touch me. We have to talk."

He sighed loudly and dragged one palm down his face, then pushed his hair back and off his forehead. "Look, if it's about the game, I know my attitude when I started it wasn't exactly the best, but I've already planned to donate all the profits to the church. I guess I got carried away."

"That's not what I meant. We have to talk." She sighed, then stiffened her back. "About us."

"Oh."

"We're not suited, you and I, Monty."

"I think we are, and you know it."

"Monty, look at you," she mumbled. "You're upwardly mobile, a businessman on the road to success."

"Yeah. So?"

"Before this I was a forklift operator. I just lucked into this job." Cindy clasped her hands together and folded them in her lap. "As if it wasn't bad enough that I've heard Robert's been bragging about me, now when everyone finds out that Robert's super secretary is really a forklift operator, he'll be so embarrassed, he'll make things unbearable for me until I'll want to quit."

She flinched when Monty's hands covered her own, then closed with a gentle squeeze. "No, the opposite will happen. Everyone will be so impressed that you went above and beyond the call of duty, you'll be even more valuable than you already are."

She raised her eyes, meeting his gaze. "No, Monty, you don't understand those people. Troy knows what they're like. When I first started the job, he warned me not to let Robert find out what I did. At first I didn't believe it, but the more I saw and heard, the more I knew he was right. I could be looking for another job very soon. I planned on going back to school at night in September, but if I'm without a job, I won't be able to do that, either."

He shook his head and squeezed her hands again. "No. This time Troy is wrong. You heard him. He said you saved their biggest account. Robert was really impressed. I was standing beside him. You'll see."

Cindy shook her head, but said nothing.

"Now I'd like to hear what's really bothering you. I can't sleep at night, worrying that I've done something to hurt you, because if I have, I'll never forgive myself."

In an unexpected move, he released her hands, reached in his pocket and put his glasses on, then resumed his position. "There. I want to see you properly."

At first, she blinked, but then steeled her nerve. She would have preferred if he couldn't see her quite so clearly. Cindy sucked in a deep breath. "How do you feel about me?"

Monty moved his head slightly and knotted his brows, as if he couldn't believe what she was asking. He waited a little too long before he finally replied. "Well, I think you know that I like you very much."

"Monty, I like you, too, but I'm not sure what we're feeling is the same thing." He started to open his mouth, but she shook her head. "Please, this is difficult. Let me finish." She pulled her hands away from him, unable to touch him as she poured out her heart. "I'm worried that even though you think you like me, what you feel is because of what happened. You know, about your accident. What you're feeling is perfectly natural, but I think you've lifted me up on a pedestal far above where I belong. I'm not an angel, and I'm not a hero. I'm just an ordinary person who was in the right place at the right time by God's design and timing."

The time he took to think about her words seemed like an eternity.

"I know that, Cindy. Is it so impossible to believe I like you just for who you are?"

She didn't know whether to believe him or not. Before she could think of an adequate response, he spoke again.

"I did a lot of praying and a lot of soul-searching in the hospital and the time immediately following. I truly believe God Himself spared my life. You helped, as part of His plan, there's no doubt about that, but I believe that God planned both for you to be there at the right time and then for us to meet again. You've got to believe me."

She wanted to believe him. She'd never wanted so much to believe anything in her life.

"Is there anything else you wanted to talk to me about?"

The backs of her eyes burned, but she held it back. "No," she croaked out in a voice barely above a whisper. She wanted to believe that he was telling the truth and that all her worries and fears were for nothing, but she didn't know yet if she could.

"Good. Now, let's see what's on television."

With shaking hands, Cindy lifted the remote and found a ridiculous show featuring people's home videos. She couldn't handle anything that required her to think or follow a story line. In the background, they could hear Troy's and Erin's giggles and groans as they played Monty's game.

Gently, Monty raised his left leg to rest on the coffee table, grimaced in apology, then tucked her beside him and laid his arm behind her on the back of the couch. She didn't snuggle in and he didn't push it, much to her relief. She still needed time to think, but not when they were together. Troy's voice echoed from the den. "I did it! I did it! I won!"

Erin squealed with glee and applauded.

Cindy frowned, remembering the premise of the game. Troy had now succeeded in wiping himself off the face of cyber-earth. Monty grinned ear to ear, then gave her shoulder a gentle nudge. "Hurry, and you'll get to see the beautiful princess."

She opened her mouth to protest, but curiosity got the better of her. Without waiting for Monty, she ran to the den where Erin and Troy were still glued to the computer screen. A prison cage lowered over the blond Evil Overlord, and the dark-haired Handsome Prince entered the castle with a key obtained earlier in the game. He unlocked the door to the prison tower, and to the electronic version of a popular love ballad, out came a beautiful brown-haired princess in a long flowing gown. Cindy couldn't help but notice the princess was exactly equal in height to the prince. A fanfare of music sounded as they kissed, a curtain came down, and the words "And they lived happily ever after" floated across the screen. Out of the corner of her eye, she saw Monty hobble in.

Erin and Troy applauded. Monty's cheeks reddened, but he said nothing.

"Wow!" exclaimed Troy. "Great game! Got any others?"

Cindy couldn't stand it anymore. "Troy, tell me, do you think any of those characters looked a teensy-weensy bit familiar?"

"What do you mean?"

Cindy could almost see the gears in his head whirring as Troy looked at Monty's face, tilted his head slightly, narrowed one eye, then grinned. "Well, that prince might have looked a little familiar, eh, Monty?" He winked. Monty blushed.

"Anybody else?" Cindy asked.

"Cindy, there were only two characters in the game until the end. There was only the Prince and the bad guy. . . ." His voice trailed off. He ran his fingers through his shaggy blond hair. "Wait a minute!" He glanced to the screen, which only showed the words "Prince's Perils" prominently against a forest background. He crossed his arms on his chest, and the corners of his mouth tipped up in a dawning grin. "Was that bad guy who I think he was?"

Monty started to snicker. "Maybe there might have been a slight resemblance."

Troy burst out laughing. "I'd ask what I did to deserve that, but I think I know the answer." He paused to wipe his eyes as the two men shared a good laugh. "I probably owe you an apology, but I think you got your revenge." Troy laughed again.

The corners of Monty's mouth twitched. "I guess you're not such a *bad guy* after all."

Troy twirled an imaginary mustache. "Watch it, or I'll send my mighty dragon after your wretched hide."

"Beware, vile knave, or I shall pierce your heart with my powerful sword!"

Troy slapped both hands over his heart. "You wound me, Sir! In the upgrade I shall return to avenge my honor!"

Cindy groaned. "Enough!"

Troy grinned. "So, got any more?"

fourteen

Monty stood next to his car with Cindy at his side as he prepared to go home. While the evening hadn't gone quite the way he had hoped, he now knew what was bothering her.

He'd never experienced such a rush of emotion or a loss of control as when Cindy returned his embrace and his kiss. If it hadn't been for Erin and Troy's untimely arrival, he would have poured out his heart and told Cindy how much he loved her. Knowing now what he didn't know then, he felt it was best that hadn't happened.

To his delight she'd told him, without prompting, that she at least liked him. Her concern in trying to protect him from his own possible misconceptions, despite the fact that she worried needlessly, made him love her even more.

He remained standing alongside his car and brushed Cindy's cheek with his fingertips. At his touch, her eyes drifted shut. If they hadn't been standing in the middle of the street for the whole neighborhood to see, he would have kissed her again. "Will I see you tomorrow?" he asked in a voice almost too husky to be his own.

"Sure. Tomorrow's Saturday. I don't have any plans. What do you have in mind?"

"Can I make you supper? I'm really quite a good cook."

Her eyes opened and she smiled at him, magnifying his desire to kiss her. "I'd like that. But only if you're up to it."

He would have run a marathon for her at that moment. "I'm only going to be in my own kitchen. It's been a week. I'll be okay. I want to do something special for you."

Her smile warmed him all the way to his soul.

"See you tomorrow, Monty."

He couldn't stop himself. He leaned over and gave her a

gentle kiss that was over far too quickly. "Good night, Cindy."

❧

Monty bit back a smile when Cindy walked into his kitchen. First she scanned the clean counter, then she studied the drain board as if she couldn't believe that he'd actually cooked the meal himself. He'd almost managed to dry and put away the utensils he'd used because he didn't want her volunteering to help wash and dry dishes, but she had arrived a bit early.

Otherwise, he was prepared. Soft music played in the background, and for a special touch, he'd set the dining room table, complete with place mats, candles, and a vase containing three roses, one yellow, one white, and one red, which he would insist she take home.

"Hi." He couldn't suppress his grin as she finished her scrutiny of the kitchen and guiltily returned eye contact. "Dinner will be ready in another half an hour."

"Something smells delicious. Am I allowed to ask what you've made?"

"Chicken cordon-bleu, au gratin potatoes, asparagus, and a green salad."

"You made that? You're not just reheating it?"

"I told you, I'm a good cook. Would you like something to drink? Coffee? Tea? Juice?"

"Coffee would be nice."

Monty flipped the switch on the coffee machine, then escorted her into the living room.

"Where's your cane? Are you sure you're ready for that?"

"I'm trying my best not to use it tonight. I'm going to be slow and careful." He forced himself to smile. "And lean on the walls a lot."

As they sat together on the couch, Monty had a closer look at Cindy. "Are you okay? You look a little pale. You're not coming down with something, are you?"

Immediately, her cheeks darkened. "No," she mumbled, "I'm fine. It must be the light."

He didn't think so, because unless it was his imagination,

she also had dark circles under her eyes, but he let the subject drop.

When the coffee was ready, she followed him back to the kitchen, but instead of going back to the living room, she lingered. "Are you sure there's nothing I can do? I've never had a man cook dinner for me, and I feel kind of strange about it."

Monty smiled. He wanted tonight to be special, and now he knew it would be, in more ways than one. "Everything's almost ready, don't worry."

It didn't take him long to serve dinner. Cindy stared at the plate before her in undisguised disbelief as he pushed her chair in for her. "Are you sure none of this came out of a box?"

"I did all the cooking myself, honest. However, I must confess. I'm not good with dessert. Dessert is just ordinary Jell-O and whipped cream."

"I don't suppose it's the spray stuff. You whipped it yourself?"

"I think you've got me there. Now let's eat."

Monty said a heartfelt prayer of thanks for the food and the company, and they both dug in. He kept conversation light and hoped she was having as wonderful an evening as he was.

"My compliments to the chef," Cindy said as she dabbed her mouth with her napkin when the meal was done.

Monty grinned. "Say that after the Jell-O."

"Never mind. I'm going to help you do the dishes. Do you want to wash or dry?"

He frowned. "Cindy, I have a dishwasher. There's very little to do."

"Indulge me. I insist."

The last thing he wanted was to put a damper on the evening. "I'll wash," he mumbled. That way he could lean against the counter and take some of his weight off his leg, and she wouldn't notice how he was struggling not to use the cane.

As they progressed, Cindy became increasingly quieter, and her face continued to whiten.

"We're almost done. I can finish up. You can wait for me in the living room."

Without speaking, Cindy nodded, tucked the dishtowel over the oven door handle, and left the kitchen, which confirmed his suspicions. He finished washing what little was there, left everything in the drain board, then hurried into the living room.

He discovered Cindy curled up in the corner of the couch and clutching a pillow into her stomach. All color had completely drained from her face. As soon as she saw him, she fumbled with the cushion, pretending she was going to put it behind her head all along.

Monty laid his palm on her forehead, but she wasn't warm. He sat beside her, quickly slipping on his glasses to examine her face. "You're really pale."

"It's nothing. Maybe I'm just tired."

"You look like you're coming down with something."

As he sat beside her, she cringed back into the couch and squeezed her eyes shut. "I'm so embarrassed. I'll be okay, really. It's, well, it's, uh, really nothing. It's rather personal." Cindy's cheeks flushed red. "I'll be fine tomorrow. Really."

He could feel the heat in his face as her problem dawned on him. The flu he could handle. Female things were something he'd never once had to deal with in his lifetime. The few women he'd dated in recent years were too busy trying to impress him to show any weakness or vulnerability, especially with that.

Monty stroked her hair gently. "Don't be embarrassed. Is there something I can get for you? Would you like a cup of tea, perhaps? I must admit, I don't know what to do."

Cindy nodded. Soon Monty returned with a cup of hot tea, doing his best to walk very slowly and evenly so as not to spill it because of his uneven gait.

He placed it on the coffee table, then sat beside her. Before he had a chance to say anything, she turned to him, her eyes glassy. He cringed, hoping she wasn't going to have an attack of female hormones and start crying on him. He didn't know if he could take that.

"I'm so sorry to have spoiled your evening, Monty."

"Nonsense, it's not spoiled. I'd planned for a quiet evening." Monty flipped on the television and pulled her in beside him. It wasn't exactly what he had in mind, but he would make the best of it. Last night, they had managed to clear one hurdle, and tonight he wanted to sit and talk to her in a quiet setting with no distractions, to explore where they were going with their blossoming relationship.

He didn't know much about women in general, but he'd overheard snippets of conversation from enough men and heard enough PMS jokes to know this was probably not a good time to talk about emotional issues. Not all women would be affected that way, he knew, but this was too important to take any chances. He would wait. Besides, relaxing on the couch with Cindy nestled in his arms was a pleasant way to spend an evening.

Cindy pulled her knees up until she was curled into a ball and nestled her head into his chest. He felt sorry for her as she suffered, but part of him enjoyed the simple pleasure of holding her, sharing a casual togetherness in the quiet of the evening.

He wondered if this was what it would be like if they got married and settled into a daily routine. A comfortable end to a hectic day.

Monty blinked hard and stared blankly at the television, then tried to figure out how much of the program he had missed, daydreaming.

He turned his head, about to ask if she wanted another cup of tea, but Cindy's eyes were closed. Her whole body was limp, her breathing slow and even. Gently, he nestled a soft kiss through the hair on her forehead. This indeed was the future he wanted.

Doing his best not to move Cindy too much, he reached for the remote control, flicked off the television, and flicked the CD on to whatever had been playing before supper. Monty closed his eyes to enjoy the quiet music and the warmth of the woman in his arms.

Monty slowly became aware of a soft movement. His eyes sprang open to discover Cindy snuggled in beside him on the couch, just waking up herself. A quick check of the time showed it was after midnight.

She blinked repeatedly, but said nothing.

He leaned back to let her disengage herself. "I think we both fell asleep. I guess that show wasn't as exciting as I thought it would be."

"Excuse me for a minute." She ran off to the washroom, which gave Monty the time he needed to wake up and to give himself a mental kick. How could he have fallen asleep?

He managed to collect his wits by the time she returned, but barely.

"It's really late. I think I'd better be going."

Despite the fact that his romantic evening didn't go as planned, Monty thought they still had a pleasant time together. "Wait. Before you go, I want to give you something." He led her into the dining room and picked up the vase of flowers. "These are for you."

"Thank you, they're beautiful. Roses are my favorite flower." She bent her head, closed her eyes, and touched the roses gently to her nose, inhaling their natural perfume. Without raising her head, she opened her eyes wide and looked up at him. "I've been meaning to ask you, why are they always these same colors?"

He smiled, remembering word for word what he'd said in his original note the first time he'd sent her flowers at the office. "A few flowers will never come close to what I wanted to say," he quoted himself, "so here's what I wanted to tell you."

He plucked the yellow rose from the vase and handed it to her. "Yellow is for the car, the place God chose to put us together." He pulled out the white one and gave it to her as well. "White is for you, the very human angel I thought I'd never find, but God put in my path once again."

He set the vase back on the table, then ran his fingers along her cheek while he handed her the last one. "And red is for the blood of Jesus, the third and strongest bond.

> If one falls down, his friend can help him up.
> But pity the man who falls and has no one to help
>   him up!
> Also, if two lie down together, they will keep warm.
> But how can one keep warm alone?
> Though one may be overpowered, two can defend
>   themselves.
> A cord of three strands is not quickly broken."

Tears glistened in her eyes. "Oh, Monty, that's beautiful."

"That's Ecclesiastes 4:10–12. This bond, designed by God, will never be broken. I love you, Cindy."

She burst into tears. "Oh, Monty, I love you, too," she sobbed. Without warning and still holding all three flowers, she threw her arms around him and pressed her face into the side of his neck. Her whole body shook as she cried.

Monty trailed his fingers up her back, then pulled her close. The flower stems stabbed him in the back and drops of water soaked through his shirt, making a cold wet spot. He didn't care. He loved Cindy, and she loved him back. He was happy.

When her crying subsided, Cindy backed up, then dabbed her cheeks with the back of her hand. "I'm sorry. I don't know what came over me. I think I'd better leave before I make a worse fool of myself."

Monty kissed her cheek, then reached for his cane. "I'll walk you to your car."

≥≈

Just as Cindy hung up the phone, Robert buzzed through the intercom. "Can you see me in my office?"

Cindy groaned and grabbed her half-empty coffee cup on the way.

Fortunately she felt better today than she had a few days ago. After she got home from Monty's Saturday night, she'd gone straight to bed and stayed there. Instead of showing up at her door Sunday morning, Monty had phoned to check up on her first, which was a good thing. She'd been so sick she hadn't gone to church, nor had she made it out of bed all day except to go to the washroom. She'd also slept like a log all night.

Today, she felt like a new person.

She paused just long enough to run her fingers over the petals of the latest vase of flowers. Yellow, white, and red.

Cindy tried not to get misty-eyed over the thought. She had feared that it would be her worst nightmare if Monty declared any feelings of love for her. Instead, the moment had been the happiest in her life, despite the fact that she'd cried her eyes out at the time. She loved him, too, and now that her worries about his motivations and interpretation of the circumstances had been laid to rest, they could date like normal people, carry on a normal relationship, and see if there was a future for them, which she had a feeling there would be.

Next time she saw Monty, this time for sure she would tell him to stop sending the flowers, only this time for a different reason. Now that she knew what they meant, she couldn't afford to break into tears in the middle of the office or sit and stare at them all day while her work piled up.

Robert dumped another massive volume of work on her, in addition to another huge pile of urgent correspondence that had to be done before she went home for the night. Cindy sighed, buried her face in her hands for a few seconds, and shook her head in resignation. It was going to be a long day.

The clock showed seven o'clock by the time she finally finished the last letter. She had just closed her drawer when Robert sauntered up to her desk.

He smiled, then crossed his arms over his belly. "We're finally finished. I appreciate your staying so late, and to make it up to you, if you don't have plans, and since it's my wife's bowling night, let me buy dinner."

She'd been hoping to spend the evening with Monty, but after playing telephone tag with him all day yet never getting the chance to actually speak to him, she knew he was as busy as she was, and he was probably still working, too. "Sure, a quick dinner sounds good. I'm starving."

As she picked up her purse, Robert's cell phone rang. Cindy took advantage of the slight delay to run to the ladies' room. When she returned, Robert was tucking the phone into his pocket.

"That was Glen. I have to talk to him about something, so he's going to meet us there."

She tried not to groan out loud. Glen Evans was the last person she wanted to see today, but she couldn't bow out now without looking ungracious.

Once inside the restaurant, Cindy expected to sit back and listen to Robert and Glen dominate most of the conversation, but instead, Glen focused his attention on her, despite her efforts to move the conversation back to business. Finally, she came right out and told Glen that she was seeing someone and was not interested. Instead of leaving her alone, he laughed and insisted that he was next in line when her present relationship ended. Cindy remained silent and left as soon as they were finished eating.

Unfortunately, Robert paid the bill and rushed off, probably thinking she was in good hands.

"I'll see you safely to your car." Glen grinned.

Cindy gritted her teeth. At five-foot-nine, plus heels, she doubted that she would be a likely candidate for any trouble. "I have to be on my way. My boyfriend is probably waiting for me at home."

"Why do some men have all the luck?" His sappy grin worsened.

If Cindy gritted her teeth any harder, she would probably crack a filling. She slipped into her car as quickly as she could, waved good-bye to Glen, and then she turned the key. Instead of the roar of the engine, only a click sounded. With a sinking heart, she realized she'd left the lights on, and the old battery didn't have enough juice left in it to start the car.

She rolled the window down. "Do you have jumper cables? I loaned mine to my roommate, and she forgot to give them back." The first thing she was going to do when she got home was have a little talk with Erin about returning what she borrowed promptly.

"No, but I'll drive you home and come back and give you a boost."

She smiled politely, even though it hurt. She didn't want to be indebted to Glen Evans when she was trying to get rid of him. "Thanks for offering, but I'm sure my *boyfriend,*" she emphasized the word, "will be more than happy to come back with me. But I do appreciate the ride home." She knew Monty wouldn't really be there, but likely Troy would, so her problem would be solved. Glen wouldn't know any better, and Troy would happily play along.

As they walked to Glen's car, he lightly rested his fingers on the small of her back, a gesture she did not care for. She walked faster, grateful for her new low-heeled shoes.

Glen made pleasant conversation on the drive, but she wanted nothing more than to get home and phone Monty.

When they pulled up in front of her house, Cindy's heart skipped a beat. Instead of Troy's car, Monty's car was parked in front. She bolted from Glen's car. "Thanks for the ride, Glen."

Unfortunately, Glen walked with her to the door. When she opened it, his fingers rested on her shoulder. Monty and Erin sat on the couch, laughing. At the same second that Monty turned his head, Cindy pushed Glen's hand away. Judging from the sudden loss of his smile, Monty had seen Glen touch her.

She turned to Glen. "Thanks for the lift home. I'll see you sometime at the office."

"You're more than welcome, Darling," he replied far too gallantly.

Cindy nearly made a scathing remark, but before she could open her mouth, Glen lifted one hand to her chin and started to bend his head, like he was going to kiss her cheek. Cindy stiffened and began to raise her hand to slap him if his slimy lips actually touched her, but he backed up first.

Cindy gritted her teeth. Even though Glen was a business client, as well as her boss's friend, he didn't have the right to make such advances. She glared at him, fully intending to have a long talk with Robert in the morning.

Instead of acting chagrined, Glen smiled, winked, and blew her a kiss before he closed the door.

Cindy seethed. She turned to Monty to say something, but his expression stopped her dead in her tracks. It briefly registered that he didn't have his cane.

"Erin said you were working late," he said, his tone low and accusing. "But you weren't working, were you?"

"No!" Cindy retorted, too angry with Glen to care that she was shouting. "I mean yes, I was working. But I went out for dinner after. I didn't know you'd be here."

"I think that's rather obvious."

Two beeps of Glen's horn sounded as he drove away, another reminder of his unwanted and unwarranted familiarity.

"If I'd known you were going to be here, I wouldn't have gone with Glen." If she had known, she would have called Monty from the restaurant and waited for him there instead of accepting Glen's ride home.

Monty glared at her in silence.

Cindy stared back. Too late, she realized that what she said hadn't come out like she meant.

Without another word, Monty stormed out, slammed his car door shut, and drove off in a screech of burning rubber as Cindy stood in the doorway, her mouth hanging open, trying to piece together what had just happened.

Erin appeared beside her.

Cindy's throat tightened. "I can't believe I said that," she squeaked out. "I've got to go after him, but my car won't start. That's why Glen gave me a ride home. I think I'd better phone him."

He didn't answer his cell phone, but Cindy left a message trying to explain what happened. Although after the display

Glen made, she doubted Monty would believe she had no feelings for Glen.

Erin jingled her keys in the air. "Let's go get your car. And don't worry about Monty. After he calms down, he'll see you're telling the truth. He'll get over it."

"I don't know, Erin."

"Everything will be okay."

Cindy's lower lip quivered. She hoped Erin was right.

fifteen

Monty shoved the door closed with more force than necessary, then stood in the center of his living room, unable to shake the sense of shock that gripped his heart like a vise. He'd listened to Cindy's voice message and couldn't believe she would try something like that. Maybe she thought he hadn't noticed the obvious familiarity that passed between Cindy and the other guy. His advances toward her had seemed so natural, like he knew they would be welcomed.

He faced the couch, where the vision of holding Cindy as she fell asleep in his arms flashed through his mind. Saturday night she said she loved him. He didn't know what had changed, but something had, although he couldn't think why. All he'd done was leave her alone on Sunday because he knew she wasn't feeling well.

He turned and took one step to the closet, looked into the dining room, and thought once again of his pathetic attempt at a romantic evening. Even inside his own home, all he could think of was Cindy. He couldn't even look at his own door without remembering how she arrived uninvited, banging on the door until she let him in.

Monty closed his eyes, his fists clenched. She was seeing someone else. Although not a violent man, he wanted to hit something to vent his anger and frustration.

Instead, he threw his suit on the bed, changed into his bathing suit, and headed for the pool, hoping that a hundred or so laps might dull his thoughts.

He returned completely exhausted with his leg throbbing, but his mind still raced. He still loved her from the depths of his soul, and he knew he always would. Unable to ignore the pangs of his heart, he flopped down on his bed, not caring about his wet swimsuit. He rested his arm over his face, squeezed his eyes shut, and poured his heart out to God, praying for an answer.

≈

Cindy sat and stared at the flowers that had just been delivered to her desk. Today it was three tulips in the usual colors.

With a shaking hand, Cindy reached out and ran her fingers along the soft petals. A few flowers had never meant so much as they meant today. Her fingers lingered on the white petals. She'd never felt less like an angel.

"What did he send today, Cindy?" Melinda's voice drifted from beside the window.

The backs of Cindy's eyes filled with hot tears, and she couldn't blink them back. She had to talk to him, but she couldn't wait until the end of the day. Robert owed her so much time by now she could take a vacation, but she only needed one day. And that day would be today.

She buzzed his office. "I've got to go," she blurted out, not caring what she sounded like. "I won't be back today."

"Uh. . ." Robert's voice trailed off. "Uh, sure, that's fine."

Cindy grabbed her purse and ran for the elevator, frantically pushing the button repeatedly until the door opened. She sped all the way to Monty's office, left the car parked crooked, and ran into the building.

She pushed the main door open too fast, causing Agnes to stop typing and stare at her over the tops of her glasses, which were perched efficiently on the end of her nose. She didn't bother asking for permission to see Monty. Instead, she turned to his office, but before she took her first step in its direction, she froze in her tracks, her heart pounding. The office was spotless, the desk was clear, and the light was out.

"He phoned in sick," Agnes said.

Cindy felt sick herself. "Thank you, Agnes," she mumbled, and ran back to the car. She knew where she was going, and she was going to do it in record time.

એ

Monty leaned back on the couch, arms and legs splayed, his head flopped backward, staring at his living room ceiling. He yanked his tie open, then let his hand drop down on the cushion.

He had meant to go to work. He really had. He was dressed and ready to go, but never made it past the living room. After being awake most of the night, he'd slept in for the first time since he started his business. On his dash to the door, he'd stopped to phone the florist before he left, and that had been his breaking point. After ordering the flowers for Cindy, he couldn't motivate himself to get off the couch.

Monty slouched forward, rested his elbows on his knees, and buried his face in his hands. He wouldn't have thought it possible, but Cindy was seeing another man. He'd seen it himself.

Bits and pieces started falling together, starting with the first time he'd seen that particular man leaning on her desk when he'd come out of a meeting with Robert.

Monty shook his head, his face still buried in his hands. He'd never felt closer to another human. They were soul mates. Two short days ago she'd said she loved him.

Monty sat upright, tugged off his tie, and threw it into the center of the room in frustration, then stared blankly at the crumpled heap in the center of his carpet.

His mental ramblings were interrupted by a knock on the door. His heart skipped a beat, then pounded in double time at the possibility that it could be Cindy. No one had rung for access, but he'd given her his access code so she wouldn't need to buzz him before coming up.

Monty hurried to the door, inwardly cursing the limp that slowed him down. With one hand on the doorknob, he drew in a deep breath to calm himself and opened it. But, instead of looking eye to eye with Cindy, he had to look down. A petite, gorgeous blond in a string bikini stood in the doorway.

He blinked twice. "Can I help you with something?" he asked.

"Hi," she said in a slow, husky voice. "My name is Sharon, and I live a few floors down. I was wondering if I could borrow a cup of sugar?" She smiled sweetly at him, then batted her eyelashes.

The woman's hands were empty, and it looked like she'd just come out of the pool, not the kitchen. Monty dragged one palm down his face. This wasn't what he needed, not now, not ever. "Where's your cup?" He made a point of looking at her hands.

"Oops!" She giggled stupidly. "Can I borrow a cup, too?"

He started to close the door. "Sorry, I don't have any sugar." However, before the door moved an inch, she raised one hand, holding onto the edge of the door, halting his efforts to close it without catching her fingers.

"I really don't want any sugar." Her voice lowered to a low, sexy drawl. She stepped closer to him, still keeping one hand on the door. "It's you I want."

Monty backed up a step, not letting go of the door, either. "I'm sorry, but you've got the wrong idea. I think you'd better leave."

He gently shook the door to get her to let go, which she did, but instead of backing off, she placed her palm in the middle of his chest. Slowly and deliberately, she flicked one button, then raked her long, painted fingernails down his shirt, moving lower and lower.

He fumbled to let go of the door and grabbed her wrist to stop her. "Look, Shirley, Shannon, whatever your name is. Can't you take a hint? I'm not interested."

"Oh, you say that now, but soon you will be. Let me change your mind." She shuffled closer and eyed him up and down, making her intentions quite clear.

Monty nearly choked. He opened his hand, letting her wrist go as fast as if he'd just been burned. "Look. Whatever you're selling, you'll have to find an interested buyer somewhere else."

A movement behind the blond caught his attention. Cindy approached from the elevator.

He opened his mouth, but before he could speak, the blond landed a resounding slap across his face, turned, and stomped off, disappearing into the stairwell.

He touched the sting on his cheek, his eyes fixed on Cindy. Her face paled, her eyes widened, and she backed up a few steps.

"Monty. . ." Her voice quivered, then trailed into oblivion. "How could you. . ." She turned and bolted back to the elevator, the door still ajar.

"I can explain!" he shouted. Trying to ignore the jolts of pain in his leg and not caring that he wasn't wearing shoes, he tried to run the short distance to stop the elevator door from closing, but it closed a split second before he reached it. He smacked the button with the heel of his hand, but it was too late. The hum of the motor signaled the start of its descent.

She was gone.

With a resounding thud, he punched the elevator door with his fist, then rested his palms on the cold metal and thumped his forehead on it.

He'd been a fool. Just seeing her, he knew instantly that the message she left on his voice mail was true.

Monty squeezed his eyes shut. God had blessed him by sending a very special woman. He couldn't let her go.

And he couldn't just stand there and do nothing. He doubted she would go back to work, so Monty went to where he thought she would go, which was her home. However, when he arrived, Cindy's car wasn't parked in its usual spot, but Erin's car was. He hurried to the door, hoping and praying that Erin and Cindy had for some reason traded cars for the day.

When the door opened, instead of Cindy, it was Erin after all.

"What are you doing here?" Erin stood in the doorway, her eyes red, sniffling, a tissue bunched in her hand.

He should have expressed sympathy for Erin being home sick, but he couldn't think of anything else but where Cindy might have gone. "I have to talk to Cindy."

Erin sniffled and blew her nose. "She's at work, isn't she?"

"No. I don't suppose you know where she is."

Erin sneezed and dabbed her nose. "Sorry, I don't. I guess you and Cindy didn't kiss and make up."

He shook his head and his voice dropped to a low mumble. "No, we didn't. Not even close."

Erin led him inside, and Monty sat beside her on the couch.

"There's nothing between her and Glen."

Last night, he let the shock of witnessing Glen's action control him. Today, he knew that Cindy had not initiated it, and more important, that by not listening to her and responding when he should have, he'd hurt her deeply and made a mess of things. "I know that, now."

Erin sniffled into her tissue, then picked up her Bible and started flipping through it. "I was trying to find something last night to make her feel better, but instead, I found this. Proverbs 27:4. 'Anger is cruel and fury overwhelming, but who can stand before jealousy?'"

Monty buried his face in his hands. He knew he was jealous, but to be smacked over the head with it shamed him like nothing else. Still, Cindy had come to him, and instead of being able to work it out, she'd shown up at exactly the wrong moment. He couldn't blame her. "I've got to find her," he mumbled between his fingers. "Erin, what should I do?"

"Beg. Grovel." Erin paused to blow her nose. When she continued, her voice dropped in pitch. "But since she's not here, all you can do is pray."

Monty gulped and stared at her. "Pray with me, Erin. Please."

She nodded, so Monty slid beside her on the couch, grasped her hands, and bowed his head to prepare himself. He wasn't good at praying aloud, at least not from the heart. He was good at making articulate and sincere prayers when saying grace and for other occasions, even praying for other people and their concerns at Bible study, but never for something that struck him so close to home. With Erin beside him, he prayed his deepest heartfelt prayer.

He recited Matthew 18:20 in his head. *"For where two or three come together in my name, there am I with them."*

The verse didn't refer to asking God for favors. It was in the context of a section dealing with strife and how to deal with someone who had sinned. And to be sure, he had sinned against Cindy. He'd put himself first. In his self-righteous anger and a fit of jealousy, he hadn't given her a chance. He'd gone to wallow in his misery instead of dealing with it, and by doing so, he'd hurt both of them. He could only hope and pray that he wasn't already too late to do something about it. He loved Cindy from the depths of his being, and he would do anything to get her back and cement that bond so it could never be broken.

His throat constricted and his eyes burned, but since he was already holding Erin's hands as they angled toward each other sitting on the couch, he couldn't let go. He squeezed his eyes shut and prayed.

"Lord God, I'm sorry, so sorry. Please forgive me, and I ask You to find it in Your heart to move Cindy to forgive me, too. And please, help me find her, and give me the right heart and the right words to say."

The tightness in his throat nearly choked him. He couldn't speak another word. When Erin squeezed his hands, he nearly fell apart completely, but he managed to compose himself. "Don't worry, Monty, she can't stay away forever. If you wait here, she's got to come home."

He couldn't wait that long. He'd go crazy. "I can't just sit here, Erin."

"Maybe she went to the mall or something."

Monty shook his head. "No, she wouldn't go to such a public place, she'd go. . ." He let his voice trail off and he jumped to his feet. "I know where she is!" He reached in his pocket for his keys, and he was out the door.

❧

Cindy sat on a fallen log, her mind blank. Birds and squirrels chirped and chattered in the trees above her. For the first time, the peace of the nature trail failed to soothe her.

She stared blankly at a spider's web in the tree beside her, ignoring the sound of an approaching hiker.

"Hi."

Cindy's hands flew to her mouth, covering a startled squeak.

Monty stood in the center of the path. "Mind if I join you?"

She merely shrugged her shoulders, not trusting herself to speak. She was too angry, both with him and with herself.

She should have seen this coming. She'd seen the perfume in his bathroom and wondered at the time who it belonged to. Now she knew. And even though it was her favorite, she would never wear that scent again.

It only hurt worse to see the other woman, who appeared to be of questionable character, leaving. If Monty would have given her a chance to explain about Glen's idiotic attempt to flirt with her, then he wouldn't have felt the need to resume a past relationship, especially so soon.

Now, it was too late. If he said one word to justify himself, Cindy wouldn't hold herself responsible for the verbal tirade that would surely follow.

Slowly, Monty approached, then sat so close they nearly touched, but not quite. A large red blotch, no doubt a souvenir from the blond, marred his left cheek. As much as it probably hurt, she refused to feel sorry for him.

"I talked to Erin."

Cindy simply nodded, then looked away. She could only imagine what Erin would have said. Erin tended to run off at the mouth. Not only would Erin have explained what really happened with Glen, she also would have reproached Monty for not believing her. She didn't know if she wanted to hear it.

She tried not to jump when his fingers rested on her shoulder. "I'm sorry," he whispered hoarsely. "I know what it looked like, but nothing happened. Just like I know nothing happened between you and Glen. I should have trusted you, and if you don't forgive me, I won't blame you. But when I saw him touching you, well, I was so hurt. . ." He swallowed hard, and his next words were barely audible. "And jealous."

His fingers drifted from her shoulder to cup her chin with one hand. "I reacted badly, and I'm sorry," he said gruffly. "I do love you, Cindy."

Cindy stared at him, her thoughts moving so fast she couldn't have put them together to form a sentence if she wanted to. All her anger dissolved into a mass of confusion.

His voice dropped to barely a husky whisper. "On Saturday you said you loved me. Do you still?"

Cindy stared into his eyes. She could tell that he was trying beyond his ability to focus on her at close range.

She couldn't help it, for all his weaknesses and all his strengths, she did love him. She also trusted him. If he said the same thing happened with the blond as happened with Glen, she believed him. "Put your glasses on, Monty."

He knotted his brows, then fumbled as he tried to put his glasses on too quickly, nearly poking himself in the eye.

When she touched his fingers, his hands immediately clasped hers. "Yes, of course I still love you. I'll always love you."

"I don't want to be separated from you like this ever again. I want to marry you, share a home together, have children with you, and live happily ever after. Please, say you'll marry me."

Her heart soared. Erin may have thought him too stuffy, but she thought he was wonderful. With Monty at her side and Jesus in their hearts, life would be wonderful. "Of course I'll marry you."

Before she knew what happened, she was in his arms, and his mouth was on hers. He kissed her almost desperately, then slowly and gently until she could barely stand the beauty of it.

He pulled away, then looked into her face in silence. The love shining in his eyes nearly made her melt. She wanted to kiss him again. She had to. "Wait," she whispered.

She unclasped her hands from around his neck, then gently removed his glasses. Holding them carefully by one earpiece, she slipped her hands once more behind his neck. "Kiss me again, Montgomery Edward Smythe."

A jay chattered overhead, then took off in flight when Monty's glasses fell to the ground.

Just when she thought she'd dissolve into the forest floor, his head lifted. "I love you, Cindy. Now let's go home."

A Letter To Our Readers

Dear Reader:

In order that we might better contribute to your reading enjoyment, we would appreciate your taking a few minutes to respond to the following questions. We welcome your comments and read each form and letter we receive. When completed, please return to the following:

Rebecca Germany, Fiction Editor
Heartsong Presents
PO Box 719
Uhrichsville, Ohio 44683

1. Did you enjoy reading *A Few Flowers* by Gail Sattler?
   ☐ Very much! I would like to see more books by this author!
   ☐ Moderately. I would have enjoyed it more if

   _____

   _____

   _____

2. Are you a member of **Heartsong Presents**? Yes ☐ No ☐
   If no, where did you purchase this book?_____

   _____

3. How would you rate, on a scale from 1 (poor) to 5 (superior), the cover design?_____

4. On a scale from 1 (poor) to 10 (superior), please rate the following elements.

   _____ Heroine   _____ Plot

   _____ Hero   _____ Inspirational theme

   _____ Setting   _____ Secondary characters

5. These characters were special because_____

_____

_____

6. How has this book inspired your life?_____

_____

_____

7. What settings would you like to see covered in future
   Heartsong Presents books?_____

_____

_____

8. What are some inspirational themes you would like to see
   treated in future books?_____

_____

_____

9. Would you be interested in reading other **Heartsong
   Presents** titles?   Yes ❏   No ❏

10. Please check your age range:
    ❏ Under 18   ❏ 18-24   ❏ 25-34
    ❏ 35-45   ❏ 46-55   ❏ Over 55

Name _____

Occupation _____

Address _____

City _____ State _____ Zip _____

Email _____

CAROLINA

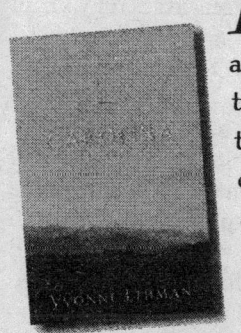

*F*amed for their Southern charm and hospitality, the Carolinas tend to attract outsiders and hold on to their natives. With the mist-covered Blue Ridge Mountains as a backdrop, award-winning author Yvonne Lehman spins four delightfully diverse tales of inspirational romance.

Here's your ticket for a refreshing escape to the mountains. Enjoy the view as God works out His will in the lives of those who put their trust in Him.

paperback, 464 pages, 5 ³⁄₁₆" x 8"

♥ ♥ ♥ ♥ ♥ ♥ ♥ ♥ ♥ ♥ ♥ ♥ ♥ ♥ ♥ ♥ ♥

♥ ♥ ♥ ♥ ♥ ♥ ♥ ♥ ♥ ♥ ♥ ♥ ♥ ♥ ♥ ♥ ♥

Hearts♥ng Presents
Love Stories
Are Rated G!

That's for godly, gratifying, and of course, great! If you love a thrilling love story but don't appreciate the sordidness of some popular paperback romances, **Heartsong Presents** is for you. In fact, **Heartsong Presents** is the *only inspirational romance book club* featuring love stories where Christian faith is the primary ingredient in a marriage relationship.

Sign up today to receive your first set of four never before published Christian romances. Send no money now; you will receive a bill with the first shipment. You may cancel at any time without obligation, and if you aren't completely satisfied with any selection, you may return the books for an immediate refund!

Imagine. . .four new romances every four weeks—two historical, two contemporary—with men and women like you who long to meet the one God has chosen as the love of their lives. . . all for the low price of $9.97 postpaid.

To join, simply complete the coupon below and mail to the address provided. **Heartsong Presents** romances are rated G for another reason: They'll arrive *Godspeed!*